Foundations of Software Testing Explained:

Manual Software Testing Book for an Agile Tester

Disclaimer:

Disclaimer: The information provided in this book is intended for educational and informational purposes only. While every effort has been made to ensure the accuracy and reliability of the content, the author assumes no responsibility for errors, omissions, or contradictory interpretations of the subject matter herein. This book does not offer financial, legal, or professional advice. The strategies and opinions expressed should not be taken as a substitute for individualized advice from qualified professionals.

Readers are advised to consult with financial advisors, legal professionals, or other experts before making any decisions that may affect their financial, legal, or professional standing. Neither the author nor the publisher will be held accountable for any loss, damage, or inconvenience caused as a result of the information presented in this book. The reader assumes full responsibility for the implementation and outcomes of the strategies and recommendations discussed.

Use of this book constitutes acceptance of these terms and the understanding that the guidance and strategies laid out are opinions of the author and should not be considered definitive plans of action. No promise or guarantee of specific results is made or implied. By reading this book, you acknowledge that neither the author nor the publisher is engaged in rendering any form of professional services to you and that the responsibility for applying this information effectively rests solely upon you.

3

Chapter 1: What is Software Testing?

1.1 Defining Manual Testing and Its Importance

Manual testing is a cornerstone in the world of software quality assurance, providing a hands-on approach to identifying bugs, inconsistencies, and usability issues. Unlike automated testing, where scripts run predefined scenarios, manual testing is carried out by a human tester who simulates the end-user experience. By executing test cases and interacting with software interfaces, the manual tester deeply investigates the software, offering a level of scrutiny that machines currently can't match.

This form of testing becomes particularly invaluable for assessing the software's user interface, usability, and overall user experience. While automated tests may quickly identify functional bugs or performance issues, they lack the ability to gauge the intuitiveness of a user interface or the overall user satisfaction. A manual tester, on the other hand, can easily discern such qualitative aspects, adding significant value to the software development process.

Manual testing is often the starting point for many organizations. It requires fewer upfront costs compared to automated testing, as you don't need specialized skills to write test scripts or set up automation frameworks. This low barrier to entry allows companies to integrate testing early into the development cycle, thereby adopting a quality-first mindset from the get-go.

However, manual testing isn't just the realm of startups or organizations with budget constraints. Large enterprises also recognize its utility, especially for exploratory testing, ad-hoc testing, and usability testing. In exploratory testing, the tester actively engages with the software without a preset plan, relying on their experience and intuition to discover issues. Ad-hoc testing is similar but usually less formal, sometimes occurring spontaneously during development or debugging. These types of testing are difficult to replicate with automation because they rely heavily on human ingenuity and perception.

Additionally, manual testing serves as a safety net for automated testing. Even with a robust automation suite, there are edge cases and complex scenarios that require human intervention for thorough validation. It acts as a complementary force, filling the gaps where automated testing might fall short.

Another dimension to consider is that manual testing provides a final validation checkpoint before software release. When everything has passed through the rigorous automated tests, a manual tester serves as the last line of defense, ensuring that not just the functionalities but also the look and feel align with the expected standards.

Despite advancements in automated testing technologies, manual testing remains a discipline that organizations can't afford to overlook. It holds a unique position in quality assurance, serving a dual role of both a foundational practice and a specialized skill that can find issues automated tests might overlook. In the evolving landscape of software development, the importance of manual testing remains steadfast.

1.2 Differentiating Manual from Automated Testing

Manual testing and automated testing are often viewed as two sides of the same coin, yet they offer distinctly different advantages and limitations in the realm of software quality assurance. Understanding these differences is key for any team or individual looking to establish a balanced and effective testing strategy.

At the most basic level, manual testing involves human interaction with the software to execute test cases and identify defects, while automated testing utilizes scripts or specialized software to perform tests and report outcomes. But beyond this elementary differentiation, several nuanced factors distinguish the two.

Timing is one such factor. Manual tests are generally slower due to the time needed for a tester to interact with the software, make observations, and report issues. Automated tests, on the other hand, can execute a multitude of predefined scenarios rapidly and at any time, making them highly suitable for regression testing where the same set of tests needs to be run repeatedly.

Another aspect to consider is precision and repeatability. Automated tests can execute the same steps with the exact timing and sequence, offering a level of consistency that's hard to match manually. This makes automated tests highly effective in catching regression errors but less so in discovering new, unexpected issues. Manual testers, with their ability to apply human intuition and creativity, excel in exploratory or ad-hoc testing where the objective is to find previously unidentified issues.

Manual testing shines in areas where human perception is critical. For instance, usability testing, accessibility testing, and testing of user interfaces often require the nuanced judgment of a human. Automated tools can report if an element is missing or if a page takes too long to load, but they can't yet reliably determine if the user interface is intuitive or if the color scheme is visually appealing.

Cost and setup also differentiate the two. Manual testing often requires less initial investment because it doesn't need specialized tools for writing and running test scripts. However, its recurring costs can mount over time due to the human resources required for ongoing testing. Automated testing requires a substantial upfront investment in tooling and skilled personnel but tends to pay off in long-term projects or projects with extensive regression testing needs.

Skill set is another contrasting point. Manual testers often focus on understanding the business logic, user experience, and general functionality of an application. Automated testers, conversely, need a strong grounding in programming to write and maintain test scripts. As such, the roles demand different educational and professional backgrounds, although a well-rounded tester might be proficient in both.

By appreciating these differences, teams can make informed decisions about when to employ manual or automated testing. Often, a hybrid approach that leverages the strengths of both methods proves to be the most effective in maintaining a high standard of software quality. This balanced methodology can lead to quicker releases, more satisfied users, and a more robust product overall.

1.3 Role of Manual Testing in Software Development

The role of manual testing in software development is both pivotal and multifaceted. While often perceived as a gatekeeper for quality, its contributions extend well beyond mere bug identification. Manual testing serves as an integral part of various stages in the software development lifecycle, influencing design decisions, facilitating communication, and ultimately, enhancing the end product.

Starting with the initial stages of development, manual testers often engage in requirement gathering and validation. They work closely with business analysts, product owners, and stakeholders to ensure that user requirements are clear, achievable, and testable. This proactive involvement helps prevent ambiguities that could lead to costly errors or delays down the line.

Once development is underway, manual testers are instrumental in constructing a comprehensive test plan that serves as a roadmap for all testing activities. This plan outlines the scope, approach, resources, and schedule for the testing efforts. By preparing a well-defined test plan, manual testers lay the groundwork for a systematic and efficient testing process, setting the stage for the success of both manual and automated testing initiatives.

During the implementation phase, manual testers are frequently involved in iterative testing cycles, closely aligned with Agile methodologies like Scrum or Kanban. They actively participate in sprint planning, daily stand-ups, and retrospective meetings, ensuring that quality assurance is tightly integrated with development efforts. This iterative involvement allows for quicker identification of issues and more timely resolutions, reducing the overall time-to-market.

When it comes to the type of tests executed, manual testers often focus on areas that are difficult to automate. Exploratory testing, usability testing, and localization testing are some examples where manual intervention yields invaluable insights. They can navigate the software in ways an automated script cannot, examining the system from the perspective of different user personas, and thereby uncovering defects that may not be readily apparent through automated means.

Manual testers also contribute by performing sanity checks before and after the deployment of new builds. These quick but crucial tests ensure that newly integrated features haven't disrupted existing functionalities, providing a safeguard against immediate, high-impact issues post-deployment.

Beyond the realms of planning and execution, manual testers play a critical role in documentation. Test plans, test cases, defect reports, and final summary reports are curated with great attention to detail. Proper documentation ensures traceability, a crucial aspect of quality assurance that helps teams understand the lineage of each test case, from requirement to execution to defect identification.

Another often-overlooked role is that of a mediator between developers and stakeholders. Manual testers frequently find themselves bridging the communication gap between technical and non-technical parties. Their deep understanding of both the application and its business context makes them effective translators, capable of articulating technical issues in terms that stakeholders can understand, and vice versa.

In sum, manual testing is not a standalone activity but an integral part of the software development ecosystem. Its role is dynamic, evolving in tandem with project requirements and team structures. As the industry continues to advance, the role of manual testing remains crucial, offering a blend of technical scrutiny and human insight that serves to elevate the overall quality of software.

1.4 Scope and Limitations of Manual Testing

Manual testing is a versatile and valuable component of software quality assurance, but it's important to delineate its scope and limitations to apply it most effectively. When correctly positioned within a testing strategy, manual testing can bring forth benefits that are hard to achieve through automation alone; however, it also has constraints that necessitate careful planning and complementary testing methods.

In terms of scope, manual testing is highly effective in areas requiring human intuition, cognition, and perceptual skills. For example, it excels in exploratory testing, where there is no predefined script and the tester navigates the software based on expertise and intuition. This form of testing is essential for uncovering issues that automated tests may not be configured to detect. Similarly, manual testing is well-suited for usability and user experience testing, where the tester assesses the application's interface for intuitiveness, efficiency, and overall user satisfaction. These are qualities that automated testing tools, despite their advanced capabilities, still cannot fully comprehend.

Furthermore, manual testing is invaluable during the early stages of development, where the application is still taking shape and frequent changes make it inefficient to write and maintain automated test scripts. Manual testing provides the flexibility to test incomplete or rapidly evolving features, ensuring that development can proceed without being bottlenecked by rigid testing procedures.

However, the limitations of manual testing should not be overlooked. One of the most obvious is speed. Manual testing is inherently slower than automated testing due to the need for human interaction. This time factor can introduce delays in the development cycle, especially if extensive regression testing is needed. It also limits the number of scenarios that can be tested within a given timeframe, potentially leaving some areas less thoroughly vetted than they should be.

The human element, while being one of manual testing's strengths, can also be a limitation. Human testers are susceptible to fatigue, oversight, and even bias, which could result in inconsistencies in test execution or reporting. Moreover, the dependence on human resources makes manual testing less scalable compared to automated testing. As the size and complexity of the application grow, the effort and time required for manual testing can increase exponentially.

Cost is another limitation. While manual testing may have lower upfront costs, the ongoing expense of a full-time testing team can add up, particularly for long-term or large-scale projects. Unlike automated tests, which can be run repeatedly at no additional cost, each round of manual testing consumes resources in the form of time and labor.

In summary, while manual testing offers unique advantages, particularly in areas requiring human judgment and flexibility, it's not without its limitations in speed, scalability, and cost. Understanding these factors allows for the strategic positioning of manual testing within a broader quality assurance framework. Combining manual testing with automated methods can create a more balanced, efficient, and comprehensive testing strategy that leverages the strengths of each approach to achieve the highest quality outcomes.

Chapter 2: The Manual Tester's Toolkit

2.1 Test Management Tools for Manual Testing

The success of a manual testing effort is often directly influenced by the test management tools employed. These tools serve as the backbone for organizing, executing, and monitoring various testing activities. They help streamline the process, provide a centralized platform for collaboration, and enable a more structured approach to manual testing.

Test management tools generally come with a range of features that cater to different facets of the testing lifecycle. One of the primary functionalities is test case management, allowing testers to create, edit, and manage test cases in an organized manner. Such a repository is invaluable, not just for current projects but also as a knowledge base for future endeavors.

Another core feature is traceability, which ensures that each test case is linked to its corresponding requirement. This not only establishes the relevance of each test but also aids in impact analysis whenever there are changes to the requirements. This traceability makes it easier to ascertain what needs retesting, saving time and resources in the long run.

Resource allocation and scheduling are other significant features. These tools often come with the capability to assign test cases to individual testers and set timelines for completion. This assists test managers in workload distribution and allows for better visibility into the testing schedule, aiding in more accurate project planning and monitoring.

Reporting and analytics features provide a macro view of the testing process. Dashboards, often customizable, offer key metrics such as defect density, test coverage, and pass-fail rates. These insights are crucial for decision-making and for identifying areas that may require additional focus. Moreover, these metrics are valuable for stakeholder communication, offering empirical evidence of testing progress and quality benchmarks.

Many test management tools also offer seamless integration with other tools in the software development ecosystem, such as bug tracking systems, continuous integration platforms, and version control repositories. This interconnectedness enhances cross-functional collaboration and ensures that the testing process is tightly integrated with development and deployment activities.

However, choosing a test management tool is not without challenges. Given the variety of tools available, each with its unique set of features and pricing models, making an informed decision requires a deep understanding of your project's specific needs and constraints. Some tools may offer advanced functionalities like built-in automation capabilities, but if your focus is primarily on manual testing, such features could be extraneous and add unnecessary costs. Similarly, the tool's scalability, ease of use, and compatibility with your existing tech stack are other key factors to consider before making a commitment. Here's a great list to get you started;

- Qa Owl – QaOwl.co.uk
- Xray for Jira - getxray.app
- TestRail - testrail.com
- TestComplete - smartbear.com

In essence, test management tools can either elevate or complicate your manual testing efforts. When selected and implemented judiciously, they serve as invaluable assets that contribute to a more effective, efficient, and transparent manual testing process. The right tool doesn't just facilitate testing; it amplifies the skills of the testing team, enabling them to deliver their best work.

2.2 Configuring Your Test Environment

Configuring the test environment correctly is an elemental but often underestimated task in the manual testing process. A well-configured environment ensures that your tests are not only reliable but also representative of the conditions under which the software will operate in production. From setting up databases and servers to installing the necessary software and hardware, the quality of your test environment has a direct impact on the quality of your testing efforts.

The first step in configuring a test environment is understanding the prerequisites, which are usually specified in the project's technical documentation. These include system configurations, hardware specifications, and software dependencies. An accurate replica of the production environment should be the goal, within the constraints of your resources. This means having the same operating system versions, the same database configurations, and even the same network topology if possible.

Once the prerequisites are clear, the next step is resource allocation. Whether it's server capacity, database storage, or network bandwidth, every element of the environment needs to be provisioned in accordance with the project's scale and complexity. Resource shortages can lead to bottlenecks during testing, undermining the speed and reliability of your efforts.

Ensuring data integrity is another critical aspect of environment setup. Test data should be carefully selected to simulate different scenarios and edge cases that the software may encounter in real-world conditions. This may involve creating mock databases, dummy files, or simulated network traffic. Wherever possible, try to anonymize and sanitize any sensitive information if you're using real-world data.

Another crucial element is version control. Your test environment should be tightly integrated with your version control system to allow for seamless code deployments and rollbacks. Being able to replicate the exact conditions under which a bug was found can be invaluable for debugging and root cause analysis.

After the initial setup, validation is essential. A series of smoke tests can help verify that every component is functioning as expected. This not only validates the environment but also serves as a good practice to ensure that future changes to the environment can be deployed and rolled back without hiccups. Make sure to document the validation process and results for future reference.

Maintaining the test environment is an ongoing task. Regular updates, backups, and performance monitoring are necessary to keep the environment consistent and reliable. Maintenance also includes cleaning up after test cycles, which involves tasks like resetting databases, clearing caches, and deallocating resources.

The environment configuration is not just a task; it's an integral part of your test strategy. The credibility of your test results hinges on the fidelity of your test environment to the production setting. Any discrepancies between the two can introduce variables that make your test results less reliable and potentially misleading. Therefore, investing the time and effort into configuring your test environment pays off by laying a solid foundation upon which effective and trustworthy manual testing can occur.

2.3 Essential Browsers for Cross-Browser Testing

Cross-browser testing is a non-negotiable aspect of software quality assurance in today's diverse tech landscape. With users accessing web applications from a multitude of browsers, ensuring consistent functionality and appearance across all platforms is essential. But with the plethora of browsers available, knowing which ones are essential for your testing can be a daunting task. Your selection criteria will have to be based on a combination of market trends, user analytics, and project-specific needs.

To start, consider the big names in the market: Google Chrome, Mozilla Firefox, Apple's Safari, and Microsoft's Edge. These browsers dominate the global market share and are essential in almost any cross-browser testing strategy. Each of these browsers has unique rendering engines, JavaScript interpreters, and CSS implementations. As such, what works in Chrome might not necessarily work in Firefox or Safari, making it critical to test on all major browsers.

Google Chrome, being the most widely used, is often the default choice for initial development and testing. However, this shouldn't excuse you from verifying your application on other platforms. Firefox is known for its strict adherence to web standards, which can help you catch non-standard code practices that may have slipped through on other browsers. Safari is indispensable for ensuring your application works smoothly on Apple's ecosystem of devices, given its exclusive presence there. Microsoft Edge, on the other hand, is deeply integrated into the Windows ecosystem and often serves as the default browser for many corporate networks.

Next, look into mobile browsers like Chrome for Android and Safari for iOS. With the increasing use of mobile devices for internet browsing, ensuring your application's compatibility with mobile browsers is equally important. Many web issues today stem from non-optimized mobile experiences, and these browsers help you address this growing need.

While these mainstream browsers are essential, don't overlook the lesser-known but increasingly popular alternatives like Opera or Brave. Although they may not have significant market share globally, these could be prevalent in certain geographies or among niche user bases. Utilize analytics to understand your user demographics and include these browsers if they are relevant to your target audience.

It's also worth mentioning browser versions. New updates roll out frequently, and while most users update their browsers regularly, some lag behind. Testing on the latest version is essential but also consider testing on older but still commonly used versions, especially if your application uses features not supported in those versions.

The idea is not to test on every available browser and version—that would be impractical—but to arrive at a representative set that accounts for the majority of your user base and the most likely scenarios where issues may arise. Your focus should be on risk mitigation: identify the browsers where a malfunction would impact the most significant number of users and start there.

Cross-browser testing is about more than just ticking off a list of browsers; it's about understanding your users and the environments they operate in. By prioritizing essential browsers based on analytical and market data, you can ensure a quality experience for the widest possible audience.

2.4 Selecting Devices for Mobile Testing

The landscape of mobile devices is vast and continually evolving, posing a significant challenge when it comes to testing. Users access applications on various devices with different screen sizes, resolutions, and operating systems. The combination of these variables creates a multitude of scenarios that your application must handle gracefully. Hence, the choice of devices for mobile testing is not a trivial matter; it requires a strategic approach to ensure that your efforts yield meaningful insights.

The initial step in selecting devices involves understanding your target user base. While certain brands and models dominate the global market, your application's audience might lean toward specific devices. Consult user analytics to identify the most commonly used devices and prioritize these for testing. These analytics can often break down usage by device model, operating system version, and even geographical location, offering a nuanced view that can guide your device selection process.

Once you have an understanding of your user base, consider the diversity of operating systems. For Android, this means not just different versions of the operating system but also manufacturer-specific skins and modifications that can affect application behavior. iOS, while more controlled, has its variations between device generations and iPad versus iPhone environments. It's vital to cover the spectrum of these variations, choosing representative devices for each major category.

Screen size and resolution are next on the checklist. The variety in these factors among mobile devices is immense—from small-screened budget phones to the expansive displays of high-end smartphones and tablets. Your application's user interface and experience should remain consistent and usable across this range. Test on small, medium, and large screens, and include both standard and high-definition resolutions to validate that graphical elements and text are displayed appropriately.

Another dimension to consider is hardware capabilities, such as processor speed, RAM, and storage. Performance discrepancies between high-end and low-end devices can be stark, affecting load times, responsiveness, and even feature availability. Including devices with varying hardware specifications can provide valuable insights into how your application performs under different conditions, allowing you to optimize it better for a broader range of users.

Networking conditions can also have a significant impact on mobile applications. Different devices may have varying capabilities when it comes to network handling, especially under suboptimal conditions like low signal strength or high latency. While this isn't strictly a device selection criterion, it's a good practice to test on devices known to have different networking chips or antennas.

In some cases, it might be impractical to maintain a broad collection of physical devices for testing. Emulators and cloud-based testing platforms offer a scalable alternative but remember that they cannot perfectly replicate the behavior of a physical device. Utilize them for early-stage testing and validation, but always confirm your findings on real hardware before drawing conclusions.

The objective is to create a device matrix that captures the diversity of your user base, along with the technological variables that could affect your application. This approach helps you identify issues that may not be evident in a more limited testing environment, thereby allowing you to deliver a product that meets the expectations of a broader audience. Carefully chosen devices for mobile testing are not merely an extension of your toolkit; they're a lens through which the quality of your application is refined and verified.

Chapter 3: Fundamentals of Test Design

3.1 Understanding Requirement Analysis

Requirement analysis serves as the cornerstone of any manual testing initiative. It's the stage where the what, why, and how of an application are dissected and understood. This knowledge serves as the blueprint for planning your tests, designing your test cases, and setting the standards against which the software will be evaluated. Therefore, thorough requirement analysis is not just advisable; it is imperative for the success of a project.

Begin by acquiring all available documentation related to the software. This includes but is not limited to functional specifications, business requirements documents, and user stories. The more comprehensive your initial information pool, the more accurate your requirement analysis will be. Consult with key stakeholders—such as product owners, business analysts, and even end-users—if necessary, to gain a more profound understanding of the application's objectives.

Next, sift through this information to categorize requirements into various types. Functional requirements describe what the system should do and include specifications of data to be input into the system, operations performed on these data, and the output of these operations. Non-functional requirements, on the other hand, describe how well the system performs a function and may include performance, security, usability, compliance, and more.

Once categorized, it's crucial to validate these requirements for testability. A testable requirement is one that is clear, complete, and verifiable. Ambiguous or incomplete requirements pose challenges in test case design and can lead to inaccuracies in test results. For example, a requirement stating that the application must load "quickly" is subjective and untestable. In contrast, a requirement specifying that the application must load within two seconds under defined conditions is clear, complete, and testable.

After validation, prioritize the requirements based on business impact, technical complexity, and dependencies between modules. Prioritization helps allocate time and resources more efficiently during the testing phase. For instance, a high-priority, complex functional requirement may necessitate more extensive test coverage than a lower-priority, simple one.

With the requirements validated and prioritized, the next step is to create a traceability matrix. This tool maps each requirement to one or more test cases, ensuring that all requirements are covered in the test plan. It also helps in impact analysis when requirements change, enabling quick identification of the test cases that need to be updated.

In essence, requirement analysis is about creating a solid foundation for your manual testing project. Mistakes or oversights made during this phase can have a ripple effect, leading to wasted effort, incomplete testing, and unreliable results. Conducting a thorough requirement analysis ensures that you fully understand the system under test, allowing you to prepare a testing strategy that is both effective and efficient. It's not merely a preparatory step but a critical activity that significantly influences the quality and success of your software testing efforts.

3.2 Creating Effective Test Plans

Creating an effective test plan is a pivotal phase in the software testing lifecycle. The quality of your test plan can directly impact the outcomes of the testing process itself. Given its vital role, it's essential to approach test planning with the attention and rigor it warrants.

The initiation point of any test plan lies in a clear understanding of the project's requirements. Utilizing the results of the requirement analysis, you can now chart a roadmap for your testing endeavors. List down the functional and non-functional requirements to be tested, emphasizing the prioritized ones. The idea is to create a bird's-eye view of what is to be achieved during the testing phase.

Next, focus on scope definition. Clearly outline what is in-scope and out-of-scope for testing. Defining the scope involves more than merely listing the features to be tested; it also entails specifying the test levels (unit, integration, system, etc.), the types of testing to be executed (performance, security, usability, etc.), and any constraints, such as time, resources, or technology, that could impact testing. Explicitly stating what will not be covered is just as important to set the right expectations and to avoid any future misunderstandings with stakeholders.

Resource allocation is another critical aspect of the test plan. Identify the team members involved, their roles, and responsibilities. Specify the hardware and software resources required for the test environment, ensuring they align with the project's requirements. Consider factors like test data setup, licenses for any specific testing tools you'll be using, and access permissions to various systems.

At this stage, also outline the test schedule and milestones. Time estimation is never an exact science, but it's crucial to provide as accurate a schedule as possible, considering all the tasks, dependencies, and potential bottlenecks. Consider the time required for each testing phase, including preparation, execution, and closure activities. Build some buffer time for unexpected delays and incorporate key milestones to measure progress.

Risk assessment is often overlooked in test plans but is vital. Identify potential risks that could hinder the testing process, such as unclear requirements, unavailability of test environments, or resource constraints. For each identified risk, develop mitigation and contingency plans. Being prepared for the unexpected not only improves the reliability of your test plan but also increases the team's agility in responding to issues.

The approach to test case design and execution is another key element in the test plan. Describe the methodologies and techniques you intend to use. Will you be following a black-box, white-box, or grey-box testing approach? Will boundary value analysis or equivalence partitioning be useful for your application? These choices should align with the requirement types and complexities you identified earlier.

Don't forget to define the criteria for both entry and exit conditions. Entry criteria establish when testing should commence, often based on factors like code readiness or environment setup. Exit criteria, meanwhile, help in determining when testing activities can be considered complete. This might be based on the achievement of a certain test coverage percentage, a specified number of successful test cases, or other objective metrics.

Last but not least, specify how the test outcomes will be documented and reported. Transparency in reporting is crucial for stakeholder trust. Will you be using automated dashboards, or will reports be manually compiled? How frequently will the status be updated, and who are the recipients of these updates?

In summary, an effective test plan is a detailed, coherent, and realistic document that serves as a guiding framework for all testing activities. Its quality directly influences the success of the testing phase and, by extension, the quality of the software being delivered. Given its significance, invest the necessary time and expertise to ensure that your test plan is as comprehensive as possible. The result will be a more organized, efficient, and insightful testing process that delivers on its promise of ensuring software quality.

3.3 Designing Test Cases for Maximum Coverage

Designing test cases for maximum coverage is akin to crafting a thorough blueprint for a construction project; every detail matters, and omissions can lead to significant quality issues down the line. While the previous stages of requirement analysis and test planning lay the groundwork, it's in the test case design that the rubber truly meets the road. Here, the focus is to encompass as much of the application's functionality and features as possible within the given constraints of time and resources.

To kick off, utilize the traceability matrix prepared during the requirement analysis phase. It links the test cases to their corresponding requirements, ensuring that each one is verifiable through one or more test scenarios. This practice not only ensures completeness but also aids in maintaining a record for compliance, impact analysis, and future test cycles.

Given that software applications often possess a vast array of features and functionalities, achieving 100% test coverage may be impractical. Hence, risk-based testing becomes vital. Classify test cases based on the impact of the feature or functionality they cover. High-risk areas that are complex or have a broad user base should naturally receive more extensive test coverage. This doesn't mean overlooking less critical areas but rather allocating resources intelligently to maximize the value of the testing phase.

One effective approach to enhance coverage is to employ various test design techniques. These could be specification-based techniques like boundary value analysis, equivalence partitioning, or decision tables that help identify valuable test cases based on the application's specifications. Alternatively, structure-based techniques, also known as white-box testing, can be used to design test cases based on the internal structure of the application. These methods help in covering paths and conditions that might not be immediately obvious but are essential for comprehensive testing.

It's also critical to consider the data aspects carefully. Data-driven testing allows you to run the same test case with multiple sets of data, ensuring that the application handles various data inputs correctly. Create a repository of test data that encompasses a mix of valid values, boundary conditions, and invalid data to put the system through its paces.

However, let's not forget the non-functional aspects like performance, security, and usability. While these may not always have direct 'test cases,' these aspects often have test scenarios and conditions that need to be met. For instance, stress testing might examine how the system behaves under extreme load, while security testing could involve scenarios that validate data encryption and user authentication.

In an agile or fast-paced development environment, it's beneficial to design test cases that are modular and reusable. Changes in such environments are frequent, and having to redesign your test cases for every small alteration can be incredibly time-consuming. Modular and reusable test cases can easily be updated, thereby saving time and effort.

Another important yet often overlooked facet is the peer review of test cases. While it might seem like a straightforward task, test case design can be complex and prone to human error. A review by another experienced tester can help catch gaps, redundancies, or ambiguities, thereby enhancing the overall test coverage and reducing the likelihood of false positives or negatives.

Designing test cases for maximum coverage is indeed a meticulous task, demanding a blend of expertise, strategy, and meticulous execution. By approaching it with the rigor and attention it deserves, you significantly amplify the efficacy of your testing efforts, ensuring that the final software product not only meets its functional requirements but also delivers on performance, security, and usability. This is the key to achieving a high level of software quality, a goal that every testing effort ultimately strives for.

3.4 Prioritizing Test Cases

Prioritizing test cases is an indispensable activity that often dictates the efficiency and effectiveness of your testing efforts. This is where you decide which test cases should be executed earlier, more frequently, or with more scrutiny compared to others. The stakes are high; incorrect prioritization can result in wasted time, resources, and potentially, defects slipping into the final release.

The most straightforward way to start prioritizing is by aligning test cases with the business objectives and the risk profile of the application. Consider the business impact of each feature, area, or functionality under test. Those that are business-critical or have a higher user engagement naturally deserve more immediate attention. Pair this business-focused approach with a risk-based model, identifying the functionalities that are complex or new and thus more prone to defects. These are your high-priority test cases.

Prioritization is not a one-time activity but a dynamic process. As the project progresses and code changes are made, the risk profile may change, demanding an updated set of priorities. The introduction of new features, bug fixes, or changes in external elements like regulatory requirements can significantly alter the landscape. Therefore, your test case priorities should be flexible enough to adapt to these changes.

You should also consider the dependencies between various functionalities and features. Some test cases may be dependent on the successful execution of others. Identify these dependencies and sequence your test cases accordingly. This ensures that any failures in the dependent test cases are addressed before moving on to subsequent tests, thus avoiding a cascade of related failures that can be harder to debug later.

One often overlooked factor in prioritization is the test execution time. Some test cases, especially those that cover complex algorithms or involve multiple system interactions, can be time-consuming. If these are high-priority cases, they may need to be scheduled in a way that doesn't bottleneck the entire testing process. This might mean executing them in parallel with other test cases or scheduling them during non-peak hours when their prolonged execution won't hold up other activities.

Data can be your ally in making these decisions. Metrics from past test cycles can offer valuable insights into areas of the application that have historically been more prone to defects. Likewise, code churn—how frequently the code in a particular area is changing—can indicate the stability of that area and help in deciding its testing priority.

Don't underestimate the value of stakeholder input in prioritization. Developers may have insights into areas of the code that are particularly complex or fragile. Business analysts and product owners can provide a clearer understanding of feature importance from a business and user perspective. By integrating these varied viewpoints, your prioritization process becomes much more aligned with both technical and business goals.

In summary, prioritizing test cases is a nuanced exercise that requires a multi-faceted approach. It is essential to balance business goals, risk profiles, technical complexities, and practical constraints like time and resources. It's an ongoing process that demands regular reviews and adjustments to remain aligned with project developments. Effective prioritization is less about going through the motions and more about continuously calibrating your efforts towards the highest impact areas. This ensures that your testing is not just a box-checking exercise but a strategically aligned quality assurance mechanism.

Chapter 4: Executing Test Plans

4.1 Pre-Test Checks

Before diving into the execution of test plans, meticulous pre-test checks are crucial for ensuring that the testing environment is primed for accurate and reliable results. These preliminary activities set the stage for the entire testing phase, much like a pilot's pre-flight checks are integral to a safe and smooth journey.

One of the first items on your pre-test checklist should be the verification of the test environment. It needs to mirror the production environment as closely as possible to yield results that are truly reflective of real-world conditions. This involves checking the configurations, network settings, databases, and any other system components that the application interacts with. Any discrepancy here could lead to situations where tests pass in the test environment but fail in production—a scenario everyone aims to avoid.

Another significant pre-test activity is ensuring that all the required test data is available and correctly configured. The data should be both comprehensive and representative, encompassing various scenarios that the application will encounter in the real world. For data-sensitive tests, also check whether the data is anonymized or encrypted as per the compliance and security guidelines.

Test scripts and cases should be finalized, reviewed, and readily accessible to the testing team. Confirm that you have the latest versions, as outdated or incorrect test scripts can wreak havoc during the testing phase. It's not just about having these assets ready, but also ensuring that they are correctly sequenced, especially when dealing with complex, multi-step tests or those with dependencies.

One task often overlooked is ensuring that all required hardware is in place and functioning as expected. Whether you're performing mobile testing requiring various devices or browser compatibility tests that need multiple browser versions, ensuring that these are ready and functional can save considerable time during the actual testing. Double-check their settings and configurations to ensure they meet the test requirements.

Since manual testing involves human testers, it's essential that everyone involved understands their roles and responsibilities. Verify that the team is well-versed with the testing tools they will use, the scope of their testing activities, and the reporting mechanisms in place. A brief kickoff meeting can be an effective way to get everyone on the same page and address any last-minute questions or clarifications.

It's also a good practice to establish your exit criteria before starting the testing activities. Knowing the conditions under which you will consider the testing phase complete can guide your efforts and offer a clear endpoint. This could be based on metrics like achieving a certain level of test coverage, a maximum allowable number of defects, or a specific performance benchmark.

Lastly, communication channels should be open and clearly defined. Whether you're using email, chat apps, or specialized reporting tools, knowing how and where to report issues, ask for clarifications, or escalate problems is vital for smooth operations during the testing phase.

By paying close attention to these pre-test checks, you position yourself for a more streamlined, efficient, and effective testing process. Think of this phase as your due diligence, ensuring that your efforts in the actual testing phase are not compromised by avoidable pitfalls or oversights.

4.2 Test Execution Workflow

The test execution workflow is the procedural heart of the manual testing process. It is where planning and preparation meet action, underlining the importance of a structured approach. A well-defined workflow helps in standardizing the testing process, reducing uncertainty, and promoting consistency.

The first phase in the test execution workflow is the initiation of test cycles based on the finalized test plans and cases. Typically, you would commence with the execution of smoke tests to confirm that the basic functionalities are working as expected. These are quick, preliminary tests that validate the stability of the build and determine if it's ready for more extensive testing. If the build fails the smoke tests, it's usually sent back to the development team for immediate fixes.

Assuming the smoke tests pass, you then move to the execution of functional test cases. At this stage, testers go through each test case meticulously, performing the outlined steps and capturing the results. The order of execution should align with the priority levels you assigned during the test case prioritization stage. High-risk or business-critical functions should generally be tested before moving on to other areas. This ensures that any show-stopping issues are identified and addressed early in the test cycle.

During the execution phase, testers will also need to capture sufficient data to provide a context for any observed failures. This can include screenshots, log files, or even video recordings of the test sessions. These artifacts are invaluable for the developers who will later address the identified issues, providing them with insights into how and why a particular problem occurred.

Parallel to functional testing, specialized testing activities may also take place. This can include performance testing, security testing, and usability testing, among others. Although these are often considered separate types of testing, they can be integrated into the overall test execution workflow to ensure that all aspects of the application are thoroughly evaluated.

As tests are completed, results are typically logged into a test management tool, which allows for easy tracking and reporting of issues. Effective test management tools also offer features like linking defects to specific test cases and requirements, providing a detailed traceability matrix that can be incredibly useful for future analysis or audits.

Upon the completion of individual test cases or sets, there may be a formal review process involving lead testers or QA managers. This is particularly important for complex or high-stakes projects where an additional layer of review can provide valuable quality assurance. It's also a point where initial assessments can be made regarding the exit criteria established during pre-test checks, offering insights into whether the test phase is moving towards a successful conclusion.

When defects are found, they are reported to the development team for fixing. Once the fixes are deployed, a re-test or regression test is performed to ensure that the issues have been correctly addressed and that no new issues have been introduced.

In summary, a well-coordinated test execution workflow is foundational to the success of manual testing efforts. It sets the rhythm and pace for testers, offering a structured pathway that takes them from initiating test cycles to capturing results, logging defects, and eventually concluding the test phase. By adhering to a clearly defined workflow, you not only improve the efficiency of your testing activities but also ensure that your efforts are geared towards maximizing quality.

4.3 Test Data Management

Test data management plays a pivotal role in ensuring that your manual testing efforts yield accurate and reliable results. It concerns the creation, maintenance, and governance of data that tests utilize to simulate real-world scenarios. Mismanaged or inadequate test data can introduce uncertainties or inaccuracies, leading to misleading test results and, consequently, potential defects in production.

Starting with data creation, you'll need a dataset that thoroughly covers all scenarios the application can encounter. This includes not only the "happy path" cases but also edge cases and negative scenarios. For instance, if you're testing a login function, you'll need data for valid logins, invalid logins, SQL injection attempts, and more. The objective is to simulate real-world usage as comprehensively as possible, offering confidence that the application can handle not just the ideal but also the unexpected.

There are different approaches to source test data. Some prefer to use a sanitized subset of production data, ensuring that it mirrors real-world conditions closely. If you opt for this method, it's imperative to anonymize sensitive information to adhere to data protection regulations. Alternatively, synthetic data can be generated to meet specific test conditions. While this approach lacks the complexity of real-world data, it allows for more controlled testing scenarios. The choice often depends on the context, requirements, and constraints of the project at hand.

Storing test data efficiently is another critical aspect. Since test data is central to manual testing, you want it readily accessible but also securely stored. Depending on the project and organizational policies, this could range from secure, encrypted databases to flat files under version control. Whichever method is chosen, accessibility and security should be the primary concerns.

Maintaining data integrity throughout the testing lifecycle is crucial. Test data often needs to be reset to its original state between different test cycles to ensure consistent and reliable results. Automating the process of data reset can be a significant time-saver, especially in large and complex projects. Moreover, as test cases evolve, the associated test data may also require updates. A version control mechanism is highly advisable to track changes and make rollback easier in case of issues.

Beyond these considerations, data governance policies need to be in place. Who has access to the test data? How is it backed up? What happens to the data once the project is completed? These questions must be addressed to ensure that data management is not just effective but also compliant with legal and organizational policies.

Monitoring and auditing the usage of test data can offer valuable insights into its effectiveness. Over time, you may discover that certain data is seldom used or that particular scenarios are underrepresented. Regular audits can help you refine your test data continually, aligning it more closely with project requirements and real-world conditions.

In essence, test data management is not a sideline task but an integral part of your manual testing strategy. It needs dedicated planning, efficient execution, and vigilant governance to ensure that it serves its purpose—enabling precise and dependable testing that can vouch for the quality of the application being tested. By treating test data management with the importance it merits, you elevate the entire testing process, making it more robust, reliable, and aligned with real-world conditions.

4.4 Real-time Test Monitoring

Real-time test monitoring is the act of continuously observing and evaluating the test execution process as it unfolds. This proactive approach helps teams immediately identify bottlenecks, deviations, and opportunities for improvement. Real-time monitoring is crucial for dynamic decision-making, allowing you to course-correct as necessary and thereby optimize the effectiveness of your testing process.

Traditionally, test monitoring was often done post-facto—after the execution of test cases and sometimes even after the entire test cycle. However, waiting until the end to collect and analyze data can lead to missed opportunities for early intervention, making the process less agile and adaptive. Real-time monitoring, on the other hand, facilitates immediate awareness and prompt action.

For manual testing, real-time monitoring can be less about software metrics and more about human-centric factors. One of the primary metrics to keep an eye on is test progress. How many test cases have been executed, and what is the rate of completion? Are the testers on track to meet the timelines? If progress is lagging, real-time monitoring can enable immediate investigation to identify the cause and implement corrective actions.

Defect discovery is another critical metric to monitor. The rate at which defects are being found can offer an early warning about potential quality issues in the application. A sudden spike in defects may suggest a problematic area in the application that requires immediate attention. Conversely, a lack of defects might indicate that the test cases are not comprehensive enough or that the testing team might be overlooking critical aspects.

Resource utilization is also important, especially in projects where human and system resources are limited. Real-time monitoring can show you if any resources are underutilized or bottlenecked, allowing you to redistribute tasks or resources as needed. For example, if one tester is overloaded while another is idle, tasks can be reassigned to ensure a more balanced workload.

Testers' feedback during the execution phase should not be overlooked. Real-time communication platforms can provide an avenue for testers to share insights, challenges, or even early results. This continual feedback loop not only helps in monitoring the general mood and engagement levels of the team but can also uncover useful qualitative information, such as the usability or performance issues that may not be immediately apparent through quantitative metrics.

Also crucial is the monitoring of system performance metrics, such as server response times and resource consumption levels. While this is often considered more relevant for automated or performance testing, these metrics can provide useful context for manual tests as well. For instance, if server response times are consistently high during a manual test, it could invalidate the timing data collected during those tests.

Efficient real-time test monitoring often employs a blend of specialized test management tools and more general-purpose communication and project management software. Dashboard views can be particularly helpful, offering a snapshot of key metrics that can be monitored at a glance.

In summary, real-time test monitoring enriches the manual testing process by making it more responsive and adaptive. Through the ongoing collection and analysis of key metrics and feedback, it enables timely decision-making that can significantly impact the quality and efficiency of your testing efforts.

Chapter 5: Usability Testing

5.1 Introduction to Usability in Manual Testing

In the realm of software testing, usability often holds a place of both subtlety and significance. While functional correctness, performance, and security are non-negotiable attributes of any quality software, usability is what truly shapes the user experience. Manual testing offers a unique vantage point for assessing usability, as it mimics the human interaction with the application, thereby uncovering issues that might not be evident through automated testing alone.

Usability in manual testing is the practice of evaluating a software application from the user's perspective to ensure it is easy to navigate, intuitive to use, and effective in meeting its objectives. It goes beyond the surface-level aesthetics and delves into how efficiently and satisfactorily a user can accomplish tasks within the application. The central idea is to assess the user-friendliness of the software, gauging how seamlessly it aligns with user expectations and behaviors.

There are several key areas of focus in usability testing. These can include navigation flow, consistency of design elements, ease of learning for new users, error message clarity, and the effectiveness of user assistance features like tooltips or FAQs. Additionally, one must consider accessibility as an intrinsic aspect of usability, ensuring that the software can be used by people with varying abilities and limitations.

Manual testers are ideally positioned to perform usability testing because they can simulate end-user behavior and provide qualitative insights into the user experience. Testers act as the first line of users, employing not just their technical skills but also their empathy and understanding of user behavior to assess the application. In this sense, manual testers serve a dual role: as technical evaluators and as surrogate users.

To conduct usability testing, the typical approach involves task-based scenarios that emulate common user journeys within the application. Testers execute these scenarios, taking note of any difficulties or impediments they encounter. Did the interface make it easy to complete the task? Were any elements confusing or misleading? Was the path to the desired outcome straightforward, or did it require unnecessary steps? Answers to questions like these offer valuable information that can be used to improve the software's usability.

When executed correctly, usability testing can yield actionable insights that lead to a more refined, intuitive, and user-friendly application. However, it's important to recognize that usability testing is often iterative. It's rare to get every usability aspect right in the first go. You may need multiple rounds of testing and refinement to reach an optimal level of usability.

In addition to standard usability tests, other specialized methods, such as heuristic evaluations, A/B testing, and user journey mapping, may also be employed. Each has its own advantages and applications, and often a combination of these methods is used for a more holistic assessment.

In sum, usability in manual testing serves as a litmus test for the overall user experience. By ensuring that an application is not just functional but also user-friendly, manual testing delivers a comprehensive quality assessment that can significantly influence the software's success in the market. Therefore, the importance of usability testing within the manual testing framework cannot be understated; it is indispensable for creating software that not only works but also delights its users.

5.2 Heuristic Evaluations

Heuristic evaluations constitute a specialized technique within usability testing, enabling an expedited yet insightful examination of an application's user interface. Originating from Jakob Nielsen's usability engineering work, heuristic evaluations focus on reviewing a product to identify usability problems based on a set of predefined heuristics or principles. Unlike typical usability tests that involve actual users, heuristic evaluations are generally conducted by usability experts who apply these principles to assess the interface.

The heuristics serve as a framework for the evaluators, guiding them through specific elements and interactions that are crucial for a positive user experience. Common heuristics include visibility of system status, user control and freedom, consistency and standards, error prevention, and so forth. These principles are intentionally broad, applicable to a wide range of interface types and user interactions, which makes heuristic evaluations a versatile tool for assessing usability.

To initiate a heuristic evaluation, the first step is to identify or adapt a set of heuristics that are most pertinent to the application under review. Depending on the type and purpose of the software, certain heuristics may hold more relevance than others. For instance, if you are evaluating a mobile application, additional heuristics around touchscreen interactions and small screen real estate may be beneficial.

Once the set of heuristics is established, evaluators navigate through the application, meticulously scrutinizing each user interface element and interaction against these heuristics. Their role is to play the devil's advocate, consciously seeking out usability issues that an end-user might encounter. The focus isn't just on identifying issues but also on gauging their severity. Are they mere annoyances, or do they fundamentally impair the user's ability to complete tasks?

Evaluators document their findings, often in a structured format that includes the identified issue, the heuristic it violates, its severity, and suggested fixes. This documentation serves as a targeted to-do list for the development team, pointing out specific areas where usability improvements are needed. It's not uncommon for multiple evaluators to conduct separate evaluations and later pool their findings. This approach can offer a more well-rounded view, minimizing the risk of oversight and incorporating diverse perspectives.

One of the major advantages of heuristic evaluations is their efficiency. They can be conducted relatively quickly and don't require the logistical arrangements of typical usability tests, such as participant recruitment and data collection. However, this efficiency does come with trade-offs. Being an expert-driven method, heuristic evaluations can miss issues that real users, with varied backgrounds and skill levels, might face. Therefore, heuristic evaluations are often most effective when used in conjunction with other usability testing methods.

In summary, heuristic evaluations are a potent instrument in a manual tester's usability toolkit. They offer a structured yet adaptable approach to identify usability issues, providing actionable insights that can materially improve an application's user interface. Particularly useful for early-stage assessments or iterative improvements, heuristic evaluations should be an integral part of your comprehensive usability testing strategy.

5.3 User Journey Mapping

User Journey Mapping is a visually-oriented method employed to gain a deeper understanding of how users interact with a product or application. A user journey map is essentially a narrative that charts the course of a user's experience, from their initial engagement with the application to the completion of a specific goal or set of tasks. Each touchpoint, decision node, and interaction is plotted, offering an overarching view of the user's path and experience.

The strength of user journey mapping lies in its ability to humanize the analytical and technical aspects of usability testing. Whereas other methods might focus solely on metrics and heuristics, user journey mapping emphasizes the emotional and cognitive states of the user. Does a particular interaction evoke confusion, delight, or frustration? What motivates the user to move from one touchpoint to another? By answering such questions, this method provides invaluable qualitative data that enrich the overall understanding of usability.

To create a user journey map, a series of steps are usually followed:

1. **Define Objectives**: The first step is to outline what you want to achieve with the map. Are you trying to improve the onboarding process, optimize a checkout flow, or perhaps enhance the overall navigational experience?

2. **Identify Personas**: Knowing your user base is crucial. Define personas that represent segments of your user population, focusing on their goals, frustrations, and common tasks.

3. **List Touchpoints**: Identify the various interaction points within the application where the user will engage with the interface.

4. **Plot the Journey**: Construct a timeline or flowchart that outlines the sequence of touchpoints for each persona, noting what actions they take and what decisions they make at each stage.

5. **Incorporate Emotional States**: Annotate the map with the emotional highs and lows that a user might experience at each touchpoint.

6. **Identify Barriers**: Highlight any obstacles or pain points that hinder the user's progress towards their goals.

7. **Suggest Improvements**: Finally, note down potential enhancements that could elevate the user experience, based on the observed journey.

Manual testers play a critical role in this exercise, often acting as the architects of the user journey map. They use their understanding of the application, combined with real-world usage data and perhaps even direct user feedback, to construct a realistic journey. Moreover, they use their expertise to scrutinize this journey through the lens of usability, spotting areas where the application may not meet user expectations or where there might be room for improvement.

The completed user journey map serves multiple purposes. It is an excellent communication tool that can be shared with designers, developers, and stakeholders, ensuring everyone understands the user experience from a holistic perspective. Additionally, it offers targeted insights for refinement, highlighting exactly where improvements are needed and what those improvements might entail.

In essence, user journey mapping extends the scope of manual usability testing beyond the interface and into the realm of experience. It allows testers to delve into the human aspects of interaction, adding a layer of empathy and context that numbers alone cannot provide. Therefore, user journey mapping complements traditional usability testing methods by providing a rich, user-centered perspective that leads to a more comprehensive and nuanced understanding of usability.

5.4 A/B Testing for Usability

A/B testing serves as a compelling mechanism to empirically assess usability variations in a live environment. In essence, A/B testing involves presenting two different versions of a particular feature or interface element to separate groups of users. One version is typically the existing design (A), considered the control, while the other (B) contains the modifications under evaluation. Metrics such as conversion rates, time spent on a task, and user satisfaction are then compared between the two groups to determine which version offers a superior usability experience.

The precision of A/B testing lies in its data-driven approach. Unlike heuristic evaluations or user journey mapping, which rely on expert judgment and qualitative insights, A/B testing thrives on quantitative metrics. This method provides a straightforward way to gauge the impact of specific changes on usability, rooted in statistical evidence. By conducting A/B tests, manual testers can validate or invalidate their hypotheses about usability improvements with a high degree of confidence.

To set up an A/B test for usability, the following sequence of steps is typically followed:

1. **Hypothesis Formulation**: Before initiating the test, formulate a clear hypothesis that identifies what you aim to improve and how you expect the changes to affect user behavior.

2. **Test Design**: Decide on the interface element(s) that will be modified. These could range from button colors and text labels to entire workflow processes. Also, outline the metrics that will be monitored to assess usability.

3. **User Segmentation**: Divide the user base into two or more groups, ensuring that each group is statistically significant and representative of your overall user population.

4. **Implementation**: Deploy the A/B test, directing users to either the control or the modified version as they interact with the application. This is often facilitated through specialized A/B testing software.

5. **Data Collection**: Monitor the selected metrics for a predetermined period, ensuring that sufficient data is collected for a reliable analysis.

6. **Result Analysis**: Apply statistical methods to compare the performance metrics of the two groups, identifying any significant differences.

7. **Decision Making**: Based on the analysis, decide whether to implement the changes, refine them for further testing, or revert to the original design.

8. **Documentation and Sharing**: Document the entire process, from hypothesis formulation to results and decisions. Share these insights with the team, enriching the collective understanding of the application's usability landscape.

The role of manual testers in A/B testing is multifaceted. While they might not always manage the testing process end-to-end, their expertise is crucial in formulating hypotheses based on prior usability findings, determining relevant metrics, and interpreting the results. Furthermore, manual testers often collaborate with data analysts to scrutinize the statistics, ensuring that the outcomes are not only statistically significant but also meaningful from a usability standpoint.

However, one must be cautious of a few pitfalls. A/B testing is not a silver bullet; it evaluates the short-term impact of specific changes but may not provide insights into long-term usability or user satisfaction. Additionally,

A/B tests need to be meticulously designed and executed to avoid confounding variables that could skew results.

In the grand tapestry of usability testing methods, A/B testing offers a targeted, data-centric lens through which the efficacy of specific changes can be rigorously assessed. It harmoniously complements other, more qualitative methods, rounding out a comprehensive usability testing strategy.

Chapter 6: Responsive Design Testing

6.1 Understanding the Importance of Responsiveness

Responsiveness in web and application design is more than a buzzword; it's a crucial framework that caters to a multitude of devices and user contexts. Responsiveness ensures that an application or website adjusts its layout, images, and functionalities to provide an optimized experience regardless of the screen size or device being used. As the computing landscape evolves to include a wide range of devices—smartphones, tablets, laptops, desktops, and even smart TVs—the need for responsive design has moved from being a luxury to an imperative.

For manual testers, understanding the importance of responsiveness extends beyond the user experience. It directly influences test planning, execution, and ultimately the overall quality of the product. In today's interconnected world, users expect seamless transitions between different devices. They may start a task on their phone while commuting, continue it on a laptop at work, and complete it on a tablet at home. Each transition point is a potential failure point from a testing perspective, making the role of responsiveness in manual testing a linchpin for ensuring cross-device and cross-platform compatibility.

The absence of responsive design can significantly impact an application's market reach and user satisfaction. Users are less likely to engage with an application if it doesn't display or function correctly on their device. Even minor issues like misaligned text or unclickable buttons can erode trust and lead to negative user reviews, which in turn affect the brand's credibility and revenue. A responsive application, on the other hand, not only casts a wider net in terms of user engagement but also creates a more inclusive digital environment, making technology accessible to a broader demographic.

In a testing context, responsiveness entails a series of considerations:

1. **Layout Testing**: Evaluating how well the application adapts its layout based on different screen sizes and resolutions.

2. **UI Element Scaling**: Checking if UI elements like buttons, images, and forms scale appropriately without loss of function or aesthetic value.

3. **Performance**: Assessing how the application performs under varying conditions, particularly focusing on load times and resource utilization across different devices.

4. **Interoperability**: Ensuring that the application functions seamlessly when transitioning from one device or browser to another.

5. **Media Queries**: Validating the implementation of media queries in the code, which allow the application to adapt its style based on device capabilities.

6. **User Scenarios**: Running tests to simulate real-world use cases where users switch between different devices.

7. **Error Handling**: Verifying that the application can gracefully handle errors or limitations encountered in various device configurations.

Given these broad and nuanced considerations, manual testing for responsiveness becomes an integral part of the quality assurance process.

Manual testers must meticulously evaluate each aspect, armed with an understanding of how device diversity impacts usability, performance, and overall user experience. Through this multifaceted lens, the importance of responsiveness is elevated from a design principle to a quality metric that directly correlates with the product's success in the market.

6.2 Mobile-First vs Desktop-First Testing

The choice between mobile-first and desktop-first testing hinges on various factors such as target audience, application purpose, and development approach. Both paradigms have their own set of advantages and challenges, which must be considered carefully in the manual testing strategy.

Mobile-First Testing

In a mobile-first approach, the application is designed primarily for mobile devices, with features and functionalities optimized for smaller screens. Given the increasing prevalence of mobile users, this approach is gaining traction across various sectors. When testing is aligned with a mobile-first strategy, the focus shifts towards:

1. **Touch Interactions**: Verifying touch-screen functionalities such as swipes, pinches, and taps.

2. **Limited Resources**: Mobile devices typically have constrained processing power and memory, making it essential to test for optimal resource utilization.

3. **Network Fluctuations**: Mobile devices often experience varying network conditions, requiring tests that gauge how well the application handles network latency and offline scenarios.

4. **Battery Consumption**: A poorly optimized application can drain a device's battery, which is another aspect that testers should evaluate.

5. **Portability**: With numerous devices in the market, mobile-first testing often involves evaluating the application across different operating systems, screen sizes, and hardware capabilities.

Desktop-First Testing

In contrast, desktop-first design starts with a rich, feature-intensive application optimized for larger screens, which is later pared down for mobile compatibility. When testing within a desktop-first context, the considerations include:

1. **Mouse and Keyboard Interactions**: Unlike mobile devices, desktops primarily rely on a mouse and keyboard. Manual testing should ensure that all functionalities are accessible through these input devices.

2. **Browser Compatibility**: Desktop applications are more prone to browser-specific issues, which necessitates comprehensive cross-browser testing.

3. **Powerful Resources**: Desktops typically have more robust hardware, allowing applications to consume more resources. Nevertheless, performance metrics still need to be evaluated to ensure they meet specified benchmarks.

4. **Multi-Window Support**: Users may often interact with multiple applications simultaneously, and manual testing should account for such multitasking scenarios.

5. **High Resolution**: Desktops offer larger screen sizes and higher resolutions, and manual testing should ensure that the application scales appropriately.

Integrated Testing Strategy

In the current digital landscape, an either-or approach is often insufficient. An integrated testing strategy that accommodates both mobile and desktop environments is usually recommended. However, the sequence—whether to start with mobile or desktop—depends on the application's primary user base, feature set, and business objectives.

Manual testers should be proficient in adapting their testing strategies based on whether the design is mobile-first or desktop-first. It's not just about the technicalities of different devices but also the user expectations and interactions that are molded by these platforms. Understanding this helps manual testers develop a nuanced test plan, contributing to a product that offers a consistent and effective user experience irrespective of the device being used.

6.3 Orientation Changes and Viewport Sizes

Orientation changes and varying viewport sizes present distinct challenges in manual testing, primarily because they directly influence how the user interacts with an application. Different orientations and viewport sizes can drastically alter the user experience, affecting layout, usability, and overall functionality. Therefore, understanding the intricacies of these elements is vital in the manual testing landscape.

Orientation Changes

The shift between portrait and landscape modes on mobile devices isn't just a trivial user preference. It can affect the arrangement of UI elements, the visibility of content, and the responsiveness of interactive features.

1. **Layout Reconfiguration**: Testers must verify that the layout reconfigures smoothly when the device orientation changes. Elements shouldn't overlap, truncate, or disappear.

2. **Functional Consistency**: All features should function consistently irrespective of orientation. For instance, a video should continue playing seamlessly when the device is rotated.

3. **Transition Effects**: If the application employs transitional animations or effects during orientation changes, these should be fluid and not result in glitches or crashes.

4. **State Preservation**: It's important to ensure that the application's state remains intact during orientation changes. For example, if a user is filling out a form, the data should not be lost when switching from portrait to landscape.

Viewport Sizes

Viewport size variability is common not only in mobile devices but also in desktop displays. Different devices have different screen sizes and resolutions, making it important to test how the application behaves across these variations.

1. **Scalability**: Testers should evaluate whether the application scales gracefully. Fonts should remain readable, and images should maintain their aspect ratio without distortion.

2. **Element Proportionality**: UI elements like buttons and links should be easily clickable or tappable, regardless of the screen size. They should scale in proportion to other on-screen elements.

3. **Visibility**: Critical content and functional elements should always be visible, irrespective of the viewport size. There should be no need for excessive scrolling or zooming to access key features.

4. **Performance**: Different viewport sizes can have different rendering needs, affecting the performance of the application. Testers should assess load times and responsiveness across various sizes to ensure uniform performance.

5. **Media Adaptability**: If the application uses media files like images and videos, testers should verify that these adapt to different viewport sizes without losing quality or functional capabilities.

Holistic Evaluation

Both orientation changes and viewport size variations are part of a holistic approach to responsive design testing. They should not be considered in isolation but should be incorporated into a broader testing framework that takes into account various user scenarios and device capabilities.

By systematically evaluating how an application adapts to these variables, manual testers not only contribute to its technical robustness but also ensure that it delivers a user experience that is flexible, intuitive, and satisfying, regardless of how or where it is accessed.

6.4 Testing Strategies for Responsive Designs

Developing a robust testing strategy for responsive designs is crucial for ensuring a consistent and high-quality user experience across various devices and orientations. Manual testers must create comprehensive test plans that account for the multiple variables that come into play in responsive design. Here's a deep dive into the key aspects to consider when formulating such testing strategies.

Multi-Device Testing

Given the plethora of devices available in the market, manual testers must select a representative sample for testing. These devices should cover a range of operating systems, screen sizes, and hardware configurations. The goal is to ensure that the application delivers a uniform experience across this diverse ecosystem.

Aspect Ratio and Screen Resolution

The application should adapt seamlessly to different aspect ratios and screen resolutions. Testers need to evaluate how well the UI elements scale and reposition themselves when viewed on different devices. Emulators and simulators can aid in this testing process, although real-device testing should also be part of the strategy.

Orientation Handling

Manual testers should examine how the application behaves when transitioning between landscape and portrait modes. All core functionalities must remain intact, and UI elements should reposition themselves coherently during these transitions. This includes validating that text, images, and other UI components do not overlap, truncate, or become hidden.

Media Queries

Media queries allow a webpage to adapt its layout based on different device characteristics. Testers should validate that the appropriate CSS rules are triggered for different devices and orientations. This involves scrutinizing the application at various breakpoints to ensure that the layout adapts as expected.

Functional Validation

While layout and appearance are crucial, functionality must not be compromised. All features should be fully functional across different devices, screen sizes, and orientations. Manual testing should include checking form submissions, interactive elements, and navigational structures to ensure they operate as intended in each setting.

Performance Metrics

Performance shouldn't deteriorate in smaller viewports or less powerful devices. Manual testers should track key performance indicators such as load time, responsiveness, and resource utilization across the entire range of devices included in the test strategy.

Regression Testing

Any change or update in the application can potentially disrupt its responsive behavior. Regression tests must be conducted to ascertain that new code changes have not introduced any issues. This is where automated tests can complement manual testing efforts, allowing for quick validation of the application's overall responsive behavior.

Documentation and Traceability

As manual testers execute various test cases, documenting the outcomes becomes essential for traceability and future references. These documents should be detailed, specifying the device, operating system, screen size, and other relevant parameters for each test case.

Creating a well-structured testing strategy for responsive designs is a meticulous task requiring broad expertise and a keen eye for detail. Manual testers must prioritize both aesthetic and functional aspects, scrutinizing the application's behavior across a wide range of conditions. By doing so, they ensure that the end product serves its intended purpose effectively, irrespective of how or where it is accessed.

Chapter 7: Accessibility Testing

7.1 Importance of Accessibility

Accessibility in the context of software and web applications refers to the practice of making products usable by as many people as possible, regardless of any disabilities they may have. Neglecting accessibility is akin to turning away a substantial user base, which not only affects the brand's ethical stance but also has tangible implications for revenue and market reach.

Legal Considerations

Several countries have laws and regulations that mandate accessibility compliance, such as the Americans with Disabilities Act (ADA) in the United States or the Equality Act in the UK. Non-compliance can result in hefty fines and legal actions, making it essential for organizations to adhere to these guidelines.

User Experience

When an application is accessible, it not only benefits users with disabilities but often enhances the experience for all users. Features like keyboard shortcuts or voice commands can be convenient for a broad audience.

Thus, accessibility should not be seen as a checklist to satisfy regulations but as a fundamental aspect of good design.

Wider Reach

By ensuring accessibility, a product becomes usable to a more extensive range of people, thus increasing its potential user base. This extends to the elderly, who may have age-related impairments, as well as people using older or less conventional technology.

Brand Image and Reputation

Accessibility underscores a company's commitment to inclusivity and equality, which can significantly improve brand image. An accessible application signals to the market that the company values all of its potential users, setting it apart from competitors who may have overlooked this critical aspect.

Development and Maintenance Costs

Contrary to the misconception that accessibility is costly to implement, incorporating it from the early stages of development often requires minimal incremental effort and cost. Moreover, accessible sites are generally more straightforward to maintain and are more robust, resulting in fewer bugs and lower long-term costs.

SEO Benefits

Many accessibility features, such as semantic HTML or ARIA (Accessible Rich Internet Applications) landmarks, also benefit search engine optimization (SEO). Search engines can more easily index content that adheres to accessibility guidelines, improving the site's visibility and rankings.

Quality Assurance and Testing

From a manual testing perspective, accessibility is not just another set of tests but a crucial layer that intertwines with every aspect of quality assurance. Testers must be trained in accessibility guidelines and should be equipped with the tools needed to carry out these tests efficiently.

Moral Obligation

Beyond financial or legal considerations, making digital products accessible is the morally correct action to take. In an increasingly digital world, ensuring that everyone has equal access to information and services is a social responsibility that organizations should willingly undertake.

In summary, accessibility is not a peripheral aspect of software design and development. It's a central component that has ethical, legal, and financial implications. Prioritizing accessibility enriches the user experience for everyone, widens market reach, and fortifies a brand's reputation for inclusivity and social responsibility. Manual testers play a pivotal role in verifying and promoting this vital attribute, thus serving both the business and the community at large.

7.2 Web Content Accessibility Guidelines (WCAG)

The Web Content Accessibility Guidelines (WCAG) are a set of recommendations aimed at making web content more accessible to people with disabilities. Crafted by the World Wide Web Consortium (W3C), these guidelines serve as a gold standard for organizations and developers looking to create inclusive digital products. WCAG is built around four foundational principles: Perceivable, Operable, Understandable, and Robust, collectively known as POUR. Here's a closer look at how each principle is integrated into manual testing methodologies.

Perceivable

This principle focuses on ensuring that all users can perceive the information present on a website. Manual testers should confirm that text alternatives exist for non-text content and that videos have captions and transcripts. It's also crucial to test color contrasts and the ability to enlarge fonts without loss of functionality or clarity.

Operable

Operability means that the navigation and components of a website can be used by everyone. For manual testers, this involves checking keyboard accessibility and ensuring that all elements can be navigated using keyboard-only commands. Other aspects include verifying that time-limited content provides sufficient time for all users and that multi-step processes can be paused, saved, and resumed.

Understandable

Web content must be clear and straightforward. Manual testers should validate that the language used is simple to comprehend and that complex terms or jargon are adequately explained. Functional components, like forms or navigation menus, should offer intuitive and predictable behavior. Check that error messages are easy to understand and offer solutions for resolution.

Robust

A robust website can be interpreted reliably by a variety of user agents, including assistive technologies. Manual testers must ensure that the website or application is compatible with screen readers and other assistive tools. This involves making sure that the code adheres to recognized web standards and that custom components are tagged with the appropriate ARIA roles, states, and properties.

WCAG Levels

WCAG offers three levels of conformance: A (minimum), AA (mid-range), and AAA (highest). Each level adds additional criteria that must be met. Manual testers must know which level their organization aims to comply with and adjust their test plans accordingly.

Adapting WCAG to Manual Testing Strategies

Implementing WCAG effectively in manual testing involves a multi-layered approach. Testers should be educated and trained in accessibility standards. Specialized tools that simulate various disabilities or limitations can be used to evaluate compliance with WCAG guidelines. Test plans must incorporate accessibility checks as a standard element, not just as an optional or secondary layer of testing.

Lifecycle Integration

Accessibility testing should be part of every stage of the development lifecycle. It starts with initial design mockups and continues through development, quality assurance, and even post-launch monitoring.

WCAG provides an indispensable framework for making the digital world more inclusive. However, these guidelines are not a one-off checklist but a continuous quality attribute that evolves with the web. Manual testers stand as the gatekeepers of this inclusivity, ensuring that digital products are not just functional and appealing but also open to all, irrespective of their abilities or limitations.

7.3 Manual Testing for Accessibility

In the realm of software quality assurance, manual testing for accessibility is a specialized skill set that requires understanding both the technical aspects of web development and the user experience considerations for people with disabilities. It's not merely about compliance but about building a genuinely inclusive digital ecosystem.

Initial Assessment

Before diving into testing, manual testers should perform an initial accessibility audit to identify potential issues. This may include automated scans, but a human evaluation is essential for detecting issues that automated tools might miss, such as logical content flow or contextual nuances in text alternatives for images.

Focused Test Cases

Accessibility testing should not be an afterthought but integrated into your suite of test cases. These tests can be categorized based on WCAG principles—Perceivable, Operable, Understandable, Robust—and should include variations for different user personas, including those with visual, auditory, cognitive, or motor impairments.

Tools and Assistive Technologies

A variety of tools can aid manual testers in performing accessibility checks. Screen readers like JAWS or NVDA, magnification software, and even simple keyboard-only navigation should be part of the tester's toolkit. These tools enable testers to emulate the experience of users with different abilities, thereby ensuring that the application is genuinely accessible.

Human-Centric Testing

While technology plays a crucial role in facilitating accessibility, the human element cannot be sidelined. Engaging with real users through interviews or usability studies adds depth to your findings. After all, compliance does not always equate to usability.

Contextual Navigation

Check if the website or application allows easy and logical navigation. This involves testing the tab order, availability of skip links, and appropriate labeling. Not just the first-level navigation but also the deeper links, modal dialogues, and dynamic elements should be accessible and easy to operate.

Form and Input Fields

Forms are often integral to web interactions, and their accessibility is crucial. Testers must ensure that form fields are clearly labeled, error messages are explicit, and that forms can be navigated and submitted using keyboard commands.

Semantic Structure

The underlying code should be semantically accurate. For example, HTML headings (h1, h2, etc.) should be used for headings, and other elements like lists or tables should be used appropriately. This semantic structure aids screen readers in interpreting the content correctly, and manual testing can verify if the code's semantic roles align with their visual presentation.

Custom Components

For web components that are custom-built and don't use standard HTML elements, manual testers must ensure that these components are still accessible. This often involves using ARIA roles, states, and properties to provide the necessary semantic information that standard HTML elements would otherwise offer.

Documentation and Feedback Loop

All findings should be meticulously documented, with detailed descriptions of the issue, steps to reproduce, and potential recommendations for solutions. This information should then be fed back into the development cycle, contributing to the organization's knowledge base for future projects.

Continual Learning

Accessibility is not static; it's an ongoing commitment that evolves with technological advancements and societal changes. Regular training sessions and staying updated on accessibility guidelines and trends are essential for manual testers specializing in this area.

Manual testing for accessibility is a multifaceted task that involves specialized tools, an empathetic approach, and a deep understanding of both user behavior and technical nuances. By giving equal weight to both compliance and usability, manual testers serve as both the gatekeepers and advocates for digital inclusivity.

7.4 Common Pitfalls and How to Avoid Them

In the journey toward ensuring accessibility, manual testers often encounter a variety of pitfalls that can derail even the most well-intentioned efforts. Awareness of these common issues, coupled with proactive strategies, can make the difference between an inclusive product and one that inadvertently alienates users.

Over-Reliance on Automated Tools

Automated accessibility tools can scan code for compliance, but they can't capture the user experience fully. They may overlook issues like poor content structure or confusing navigation pathways that manual testing can catch. The balanced approach involves an initial automated scan followed by rigorous manual testing.

Ignoring Keyboard Navigation

Failure to test for keyboard navigation is a glaring omission. Many assistive technologies rely on keyboard-only input, so neglecting this aspect can render a site practically unusable for some users. Make sure to test all interactive elements, including forms, buttons, and links, to ensure they are keyboard-accessible.

Inadequate Testing for Screen Readers

Screen readers like JAWS and NVDA interpret webpage content for visually impaired users. Manual testers should actively engage with these technologies to validate that semantic HTML elements are used correctly and that ARIA labels are appropriate.

Poorly Defined Focus Indicators

The visual focus indicator should be clearly visible when navigating through a site using keyboard input. Often, this focus is either poorly defined or entirely missing. Check for clear and consistent focus styles that aid navigation without being obtrusive.

Incomplete Alt Text or Redundant Labelling

Alt text for images and other non-text elements should be descriptive but concise, aiding in the understanding of the content. Be wary of vague or redundant alt text that adds little value. Similarly, interactive elements should have meaningful names or labels that clearly indicate their function.

Disregarding Dynamic Content

With the advent of AJAX and other dynamic web technologies, content can change without a page reload. These dynamic changes must be announced to assistive technologies. Employ ARIA live regions or similar techniques to ensure that screen readers can capture and announce these changes.

Overcomplicating Forms

Complex forms that lack clear structure and labeling can be difficult for anyone to navigate but are especially so for users relying on screen readers. Ensure that all form fields have descriptive labels, and group related fields together using fieldsets and legends.

Failing to Test for Multiple Browsers and Devices

Different browsers and devices have varying levels of support for accessibility features. What works on one platform may not be effective on another. Ensure your test strategy covers multiple combinations of browsers and devices, including mobile.

Not Factoring in Cognitive Impairments

Accessibility doesn't solely pertain to physical disabilities. Cognitive impairments like dyslexia or attention deficit disorders also require consideration. Use straightforward language, provide clear instructions, and offer alternative methods of interaction where possible.

Lack of Documentation and Reporting

Not documenting accessibility issues with the level of detail they require can result in ineffective remediation. Clearly indicate the problem, how to reproduce it, and potential ways to resolve it. Detailed documentation is also invaluable for audits and future reference.

Neglecting Ongoing Maintenance

Accessibility is not a one-and-done deal; it's an ongoing commitment. After resolving identified issues, continue to monitor for accessibility as part of your regular testing cycles and update your testing strategies to reflect new best practices.

Being forewarned is being forearmed. By recognizing these pitfalls and integrating the strategies to avoid them into your testing protocols, you become a proactive force in the creation of more accessible, inclusive digital spaces.

Chapter 8: The Documentation Paradigm

8.1 Importance of Comprehensive Documentation

In the world of manual testing, the phrase "if it's not documented, it didn't happen" holds particular significance. Comprehensive documentation serves as the backbone of any testing process, from the initial planning stages to the final wrap-up. Not only does it maintain the integrity of the test process but also ensures that the entire team, from developers to project managers, has access to the critical data they need.

Accountability and Traceability

Quality assurance is a multi-step, iterative process that often involves various stakeholders. Having an exhaustive set of documentation aids in traceability. This means that for every defect or issue, you can trace back to the specific test case and, eventually, to the requirement it aims to validate. It provides a transparent history of what was tested, the results of the test, and any ensuing actions. This is especially important when you need to justify the time and resources spent on testing activities.

Reproducibility

Inconsistent test results can throw a wrench into your quality assurance process. Comprehensive documentation that outlines each test case in detail, including the environment setup, steps to reproduce, and expected outcomes, allows for reproducibility. This means that if a defect is discovered, the developer can follow the same steps outlined in the documentation to reproduce the issue, thereby making it easier to diagnose and fix.

Knowledge Transfer and Team Scalability

Project teams often evolve. Staff may come and go, or you might need to scale your team rapidly to meet project demands. When you have all your test plans, cases, and procedures well-documented, onboarding new team members becomes significantly easier. They can quickly get up to speed by reviewing the existing documentation, thereby reducing the time it takes for them to become productive members of the team.

Client and Stakeholder Communication

In many projects, especially those following a waterfall model, sign-offs on testing activities are often required. Clear and detailed documentation can be presented to stakeholders as proof of completed work. It also helps in setting the right expectations; stakeholders know exactly what has been tested and what the results are, removing ambiguity from the process.

Compliance and Auditing

Certain industries are subject to stringent regulations and audits. In such scenarios, comprehensive documentation is not just useful; it's mandatory. For example, the healthcare industry must comply with standards like HIPAA in the United States. Documenting your test activities, results, and compliance checks can help during external audits and ensure that you are meeting all legal and contractual obligations.

Quality Metrics and Improvement

Documentation serves as an archive of historical data, offering insights into testing cycles, defect density, and areas that might need more attention. This data can be used for analytics to draw out quality metrics, which, in turn, serve as a basis for continuous improvement.

Facilitating Automation

While not an immediate concern for manual testing, well-documented test cases can also provide a solid foundation should the team decide to incorporate automated testing. Automation scripts require a precise set of conditions and actions, which can be accurately defined through comprehensive manual test documentation.

To underestimate the importance of comprehensive documentation in manual testing is to compromise on the quality and integrity of the entire testing process. It serves multiple strategic and practical purposes, making it indispensable for achieving high-quality deliverables.

8.2 Tools for Effective Documentation

The landscape of software testing is replete with tools that facilitate documentation. These tools can be categorized based on their functions: test management, defect tracking, collaborative documentation, and version control, among others. Selecting the right combination of tools can significantly enhance your team's efficiency and the quality of the testing process.

Test Management Tools

For handling test cases, test plans, and reports, a good test management tool is invaluable. Options like QaOwl, TestRail, and qTest offer robust features that enable you to create, manage, and track test cases. They often integrate with other tools in your software development life cycle, offering a comprehensive view of the testing landscape.

Defect Tracking Tools

Once a defect is identified, it needs to be logged, monitored, and tracked until resolution. Jira, Bugzilla, and Mantis are well-known defect tracking tools that allow you to categorize issues, assign them, and track their status. Integration with test management tools is a common feature, enabling seamless data flow.

Collaborative Documentation Tools

The complexity of today's projects often requires team collaboration. Tools like Confluence or Microsoft SharePoint facilitate this by offering a centralized repository for all project-related documentation. These platforms support real-time collaboration, thereby keeping everyone on the same page—quite literally.

Version Control Systems

While not strictly a documentation tool, version control systems like Git or Subversion play a crucial role in managing versions of your test cases, scripts, and other artifacts. Being able to revert to a previous version or compare changes over time adds an extra layer of security and control to your documentation.

API Documentation Tools

For projects that include API testing, specialized tools such as Postman or Swagger offer dedicated functionalities for documenting API test cases. These tools allow you to create, execute, and save API requests, thereby documenting the test as you go.

Note-Taking Tools

Sometimes, the best tool is the simplest one. Note-taking applications like Microsoft OneNote or Evernote can be surprisingly effective for capturing quick thoughts, test ideas, or specific details that may not fit neatly into more structured tools.

Automation for Documentation

While the focus here is on manual testing, it's worth noting that there are tools to automatically generate documentation from code annotations or comments. Tools like Doxygen or Javadoc can produce technical documentation that is directly tied to the codebase, ensuring consistency.

Reporting Tools

Finally, tools like Tableau or custom dashboards within your test management system can help compile the collected data into meaningful reports. Visualizing this data aids in quicker interpretation and decision-making, providing stakeholders with a snapshot of test progress and quality metrics.

Remember, the most expensive tool is not always the best fit for your project. Consider the specific needs of your team, the scale of your project, and your long-term objectives. Effective documentation relies not just on the quality of the content but also on the robustness of the tools that store and manage it.

8.3 Traceability Matrices

A traceability matrix, often referred to as a Requirements Traceability Matrix (RTM), is an integral component in the documentation portfolio of manual testing. Essentially a table or a grid, this document links requirements with corresponding test cases, ensuring that every requirement has been verified and validated through testing. In an industry where it's paramount to ensure that customer requirements have been faithfully implemented, the role of a traceability matrix is indispensable.

What Goes Into a Traceability Matrix

Typically, an RTM is structured to include columns for requirement IDs, requirement descriptions, test case IDs, test case descriptions, and status of the test cases (e.g., Pass, Fail, Not Executed). In more advanced settings, it might also include the priority of requirements, the type of test (functional, integration, etc.), and even the risk level associated with each requirement.

Bridging the Gaps

The primary function of a traceability matrix is to offer a bridge between requirements and test cases. When a stakeholder questions whether a particular requirement has been tested, a quick glance at the matrix provides a definitive answer. If gaps exist, they are immediately evident, prompting further action.

Accountability and Transparency

Accountability is hard to enforce without clear traceability. With an RTM, it becomes straightforward to determine where a problem originates. If a test fails, it's easier to trace back to the specific requirement that wasn't met. This form of backward traceability is just as important for developers as it is for testers.

Risk Management

When you lay out all the requirements and their corresponding test cases, it's easier to identify high-risk areas that need more attention. You can color-code or annotate the RTM to highlight these risky elements, thereby turning it into a rudimentary but effective risk assessment tool.

Change Management

Software development is a dynamic process; requirements may change, get added, or even get dropped. An up-to-date traceability matrix allows you to navigate through these changes smoothly. When a requirement changes, you can quickly identify the affected test cases and adapt your testing strategy accordingly.

Audit Preparedness

Compliance audits often require detailed evidence to prove that all requirements have been tested. An RTM serves as that proof. It can be a lifesaver during stringent audits, providing a single, consolidated view of the testing landscape.

Facilitating Impact Analysis

A comprehensive traceability matrix not only shows that each requirement has a corresponding test case but also can be used to evaluate the impact of a change in one area on other interconnected areas. For example, if a particular module of the application undergoes a significant change, the traceability matrix helps identify all the test cases that need to be re-executed, saving valuable time and resources.

Complexity and Maintenance

While the benefits of having an RTM are manifold, it's important to acknowledge that maintaining a traceability matrix for a complex project can be time-consuming. Automated solutions integrated with test management tools can alleviate this to some extent, but the core responsibility lies with the testing team to keep it up-to-date.

A well-maintained traceability matrix is more than just a grid; it's a dynamic document that evolves with your project, providing structure and clarity to your testing endeavors.

8.4 Customized Reporting Techniques

In the realm of manual testing, reporting is not just a final step but an ongoing process that can offer insights, guide decision-making, and influence project trajectories. The one-size-fits-all approach to reporting is often less effective than tailored methods adapted to the specific needs of a project or organization. Customized reporting techniques can align closely with various goals, be it stakeholder communication, compliance audits, or internal evaluations. Here's how to craft reporting techniques that resonate with your objectives.

Know Your Audience

The first rule in customized reporting is understanding the needs and expectations of your audience. A technical team may appreciate detailed defect logs, while stakeholders may want a high-level overview. Understand who your audience is and tailor the report to meet their expectations.

Define Key Metrics

Identify the key performance indicators (KPIs) that most accurately reflect the objectives of the testing phase. It could be defect density, pass-fail ratios, or code coverage. Once defined, focus your reporting around these metrics.

Dynamic Dashboards

Modern test management tools often come with dashboard capabilities where you can create customized views. These dashboards can be interactive, allowing users to drill down for more details. Use this feature to develop dashboards tailored for different audiences, emphasizing the information most relevant to them.

Graphical Representations

Sometimes, a graphical representation speaks louder than numbers. Charts, graphs, and heat maps can make a significant impact, especially when you're dealing with large data sets or trying to illustrate trends over time. However, ensure that your graphical elements are easy to interpret and are not misleading.

Templated Reports

Templates can save a considerable amount of time, but make sure they're flexible. A rigid template could force you into a reporting structure that doesn't adequately address the unique aspects of your project. Always keep room for customization within your templates.

Narrative Reporting

There are times when numbers and charts alone can't capture the nuances of a testing phase. In such cases, a narrative report, written in plain language, can be an invaluable addition. This could include observations, challenges encountered, and recommendations for future action.

Scheduled Reporting

Customization isn't just about content; it's also about timing. For long-term projects, scheduled weekly or bi-weekly reports can keep the team and stakeholders updated regularly. For high-priority or fast-paced projects, daily end-of-day reports might be more appropriate.

Real-time Reporting

Real-time reports pull the latest data, offering an up-to-the-minute status of the project. While they're incredibly useful for internal team monitoring, they can also be shared with stakeholders who desire a continuous update.

Hybrid Reporting

Combining different formats can sometimes yield the best results. For instance, a summarized email report could be supplemented with a detailed attachment for those who wish to delve deeper. Alternatively, a dashboard link could be shared alongside a narrative summary, offering both a high-level view and the option for a deep dive.

Data Integration

Many test management tools offer integrations with other software like Jira or Slack, which can be used to customize how and where the reports are delivered. You could have a Slack bot send real-time metrics to a dedicated channel, or use Jira to automatically update stakeholders when certain milestones are reached.

Customized reporting techniques offer a granular approach to information dissemination, allowing you to maximize the impact and utility of your reports. By tailoring the reporting process, you empower your team and stakeholders to derive actionable insights, thereby contributing to more informed decision-making.

Chapter 9: Communication and Collaboration

9.1 Tester-Developer Communication Best Practices

Effective communication between testers and developers is a cornerstone of successful software projects. While both roles aim for a quality product, their approaches and priorities can differ significantly. However, these differences are not hindrances but complementary aspects that, when coordinated well, result in a well-rounded software product. Here are some best practices to optimize tester-developer communication.

Clarity and Precision

One of the key attributes of effective communication is clarity. Whether you're logging a defect or discussing a feature implementation, the information should be presented clearly and precisely. Avoid vague statements that can lead to misunderstandings; instead, opt for specifics that can be actioned upon.

Constructive Feedback

Criticism should be constructive and aimed at improving the product, not belittling efforts. While testers are tasked with identifying issues, the feedback loop should be couched in terms that focus on resolution, not fault-finding. This fosters a positive environment where team members work collaboratively toward a shared goal.

Regular Synchronization Meetings

Scheduled meetings, whether daily stand-ups or weekly catch-ups, provide a structured platform for direct dialogue. During these sessions, any ambiguities in requirements, updates on issue resolution, or plans for upcoming testing phases can be discussed, thus ensuring everyone is on the same page.

Utilize Issue Tracking Systems Effectively

Most teams use issue tracking systems like Jira to manage their development and testing workflow. The system can serve as a centralized hub for all communications related to a particular issue. Testers should log defects with adequate detail, and developers can use the same platform to ask for clarifications or provide updates on resolutions.

Code Reviews Involving Testers

While not traditionally part of their role, involving testers in code reviews can provide valuable insights. Testers bring a different perspective to the table, focusing on how the code will interact with other components and the end-user. This enhances the quality of reviews and fosters mutual respect between testers and developers.

Shared Documentation

Documentation isn't solely the realm of testers or developers; it's a collaborative effort. Both testers and developers should have access to key documents, such as requirements, design specifications, and test plans. This ensures that both parties are aligned in their understanding of what needs to be achieved.

Be Mindful of Communication Channels

Emails, chat messages, and face-to-face communications each have their pros and cons. Be mindful of the medium you choose for different types of interactions. Quick clarifications might be best suited for instant messaging, while complex issues could warrant a detailed email or an in-person meeting.

Active Listening and Open Questions

Whether in meetings or written communications, active listening is crucial. Always give the other party your full attention and ask open questions to encourage dialogue. This can reveal hidden assumptions or issues that haven't yet come to light.

Time-Zone and Cultural Sensitivity

For distributed teams, be conscious of time-zone differences and try to schedule meetings at a convenient time for all parties involved. Also, recognize that cultural differences may influence communication styles, and be prepared to adapt your approach accordingly.

End-to-End Traceability

Incorporate mechanisms for end-to-end traceability from requirements to deployment. This can be facilitated through software tools and enhances transparency in the process. It allows both testers and developers to understand the status and context of any task at any given time.

Effective communication between testers and developers doesn't just reduce errors and rework; it contributes to a more satisfying and productive work environment. By adopting these best practices, you can facilitate seamless collaboration between two pivotal roles in the software development lifecycle.

9.2 Internal Team Communication

Internal team communication is the unsung hero of any successful testing project. It's the adhesive that binds the various roles within a testing team, ensuring that everyone contributes their best toward the common goal of software quality. Poor internal communication, on the other hand, can stymie progress, lead to duplicated efforts, and result in subpar test outcomes. Given its critical role, here are some best practices for optimizing internal team communication.

Clearly Defined Roles and Responsibilities

Before a project starts, it's important to clarify who is responsible for what. Knowing one's role within a larger context helps streamline communication and allows team members to take ownership of their tasks. Use tools like RACI matrices to spell out roles and responsibilities clearly.

Frequent Status Updates

The pace of software development has accelerated, and testing needs to keep up. Frequent status updates, which could be daily or even more frequent for agile teams, help keep everyone aligned. The updates needn't be lengthy; a quick rundown of what has been done, what's in progress, and any roadblocks can suffice.

Effective Use of Communication Tools

The market is replete with communication tools designed to facilitate better internal conversations. Whether it's a channel-based messaging platform like Slack, video conferencing tools like Zoom, or collaboration software like Confluence, leveraging the right tools can significantly improve team communication.

Feedback Mechanisms

A healthy internal communication strategy involves both upward and downward feedback. Team members should feel comfortable providing feedback during retrospectives or other forums. The aim is to continually improve processes and relationships, and that's not possible without honest, constructive feedback.

Streamlined Documentation

Documentation can be a powerful tool for internal communication. Well-maintained documentation can serve as a single source of truth, eliminating the need for repetitive clarification. Use shared drives or project management tools to make important documents accessible to all team members.

Conflict Resolution Protocols

In any team, conflicts are inevitable. What matters is how effectively they are resolved. Having a set protocol for conflict resolution ensures that disputes are settled constructively. This can be as simple as a chain of command for escalating issues or as complex as a formal mediation process.

On-Demand Training

Sometimes, communication issues arise from a lack of understanding of specific tools or processes. On-demand training resources can bridge this gap. Create a repository of how-to guides, FAQs, or even video tutorials that team members can refer to, thus eliminating misunderstandings that could affect communication.

Process Consistency

Consistency in process ensures that team members know what to expect, which in turn reduces ambiguity in communication. Whether it's the format of status reports, the frequency of meetings, or the way tasks are assigned, consistency can enhance the clarity of team interactions.

Task Management Systems

Task management systems serve a dual purpose: they help in planning and tracking tasks, and they also facilitate communication around these tasks. All relevant communications regarding a specific task can be logged in one place, making it easy to trace the history of decisions and actions.

Informal Communication Channels

Not all internal communication needs to be formal and project-centric. Casual conversations, whether during coffee breaks or through informal chat channels, can also contribute to a cohesive team environment. Such interactions often surface valuable insights and foster a culture of openness.

Good internal team communication is a blend of structured, formal interactions and the more fluid, informal ones. By employing these best practices, you enable a collaborative atmosphere where everyone is empowered to contribute their best, making the road to software quality a collective journey rather than a solo endeavor.

9.3 Cross-Functional Team Dynamics

Navigating cross-functional team dynamics is an art in itself. Testers don't work in isolation; they interact with developers, business analysts, project managers, and sometimes even customers. Each of these roles comes with its own set of priorities, jargon, and viewpoints. The challenge is to foster a collaborative ethos where all functions work cohesively towards the shared objective of delivering a quality product. Here's how to manage these dynamics efficiently.

Establish a Common Language

One of the first steps in bridging the gap between different functions is to establish a common language. This doesn't mean you have to create a lexicon but ensuring that key terms are understood universally prevents misunderstandings. This is particularly important when discussing project requirements, quality criteria, and success metrics.

Shared Goals and Objectives

For a team to function cohesively, everyone must be aligned towards a common goal. This could be a project milestone, a quality target, or a release date. When all functions have a shared vision, the incentive for collaboration increases, reducing functional silos.

Stakeholder Mapping

Understanding who the key stakeholders are and what their interests and concerns may be is crucial for effective cross-functional communication. Stakeholder mapping exercises can be beneficial here. They help in tailoring communication strategies to suit the information needs of different stakeholder groups.

Transparency and Openness

A transparent work environment encourages open dialogue between different functions. Whether it's sharing test results with developers or discussing project timelines with project managers, the key is to ensure that relevant information is made available to all parties proactively.

Inclusive Decision-Making

Inclusion is not just a moral imperative but also a business necessity. Decisions that are made collectively, factoring in the insights from all functions, tend to be more robust and easier to implement. Use techniques like the MoSCoW method or weighted scoring models to facilitate inclusive decision-making.

Role of Facilitators

In cross-functional settings, the role of a facilitator can be invaluable. This could be a scrum master in an agile team or a project manager in a more traditional setting. Facilitators help in smoothing over conflicts, aligning priorities, and ensuring that communication flows freely between different functions.

Accountability Structures

Without clear accountability, cross-functional teams can become a setting where tasks fall between the cracks. Implementing clear accountability structures, possibly aided by tools like RACI matrices, ensures that everyone knows their role and responsibilities, thereby reducing ambiguities.

Process and Workflow Understanding

A clear understanding of the processes and workflows of different functions can enhance cross-functional communication. Testers should understand the basics of development cycles, and developers should have an understanding of the testing process. This mutual understanding facilitates more effective discussions and problem-solving.

Metrics and Reporting

Use cross-functional metrics that reflect the contributions and impact of all functions involved. This could range from defect density metrics to customer satisfaction scores. Reports based on these metrics should be shared across the team to build a collective sense of achievement or urgency, as the case may be.

Escalation Mechanisms

Despite best efforts, conflicts and blockers will arise. Have a clear escalation mechanism in place. Knowing how and when to escalate an issue provides a safety net and ensures that problems are addressed before they escalate into crises.

Mastering the dynamics of a cross-functional team takes time, patience, and strategic effort. However, the benefits are well worth it. Effective cross-functional teams not only deliver quality products but also provide a rewarding work environment where every skill set is valued and every voice is heard.

9.4 Client Communication Skills

Client communication is a nuanced skill set that software testers should not underestimate. The relationship between the client and the testing team significantly influences the project's success, especially as it's often the testers who identify issues that could delay deadlines or necessitate changes in scope. Effectively communicating these challenges to the client can make the difference between a project that flounders and one that excels. Here's a deep dive into cultivating effective client communication skills.

Initial Alignment Meetings

The project's success starts with initial alignment meetings. These meetings serve to understand the client's expectations, timelines, and quality criteria. This foundational understanding will set the tone for all subsequent interactions, ensuring you speak the same language and have the same objectives in sight.

Contextual Understanding

It's imperative to understand the client's industry, business model, and even their competition. This understanding allows you to frame your communication in a context that the client finds relatable, making your updates and concerns more impactful.

Regular Updates and Check-Ins

Consistent communication is key. Scheduled updates, whether weekly or bi-weekly, offer a structured forum for discussing progress, challenges, and any changes in scope or timeline. These check-ins provide a recurring opportunity to align your efforts with client expectations.

Clarity and Precision

When communicating with clients, the message should be clear and devoid of jargon unless you're certain the client understands the technical terms.

Ambiguities can lead to misunderstandings and set wrong expectations. When in doubt, opt for clarity over complexity.

Tactful Honesty

Issues will inevitably arise during the testing process. How you communicate these issues to the client can dramatically influence their perception of the project's success. Honesty is crucial, but it must be tactful. Frame challenges as opportunities for improvement, and always accompany problem statements with potential solutions.

Active Listening

Client communication isn't just about conveying your points effectively; it's also about listening. Active listening involves not just hearing what is said but also interpreting the underlying concerns or questions. Responding in a manner that addresses those underlying issues can elevate the quality of the dialogue.

Written vs Verbal Communication

Different types of communication may be suitable for different scenarios. While emails provide a written record and are excellent for detailed technical discussions, verbal communication, whether via phone calls or video conferencing, may be more effective for resolving conflicts or brainstorming sessions. Know when to use which method for maximum impact.

Managing Expectations

One of the most critical aspects of client communication is managing expectations. Make sure to set realistic milestones and keep the client updated on any factors that might influence timelines or outcomes. Transparency in this regard can prevent future conflicts and dissatisfaction.

Responsive and Accessible

In an age of instant messaging and rapid email exchanges, responsiveness can significantly influence the client's perception of your reliability. Whether it's a quick acknowledgment of a received message or a more detailed response, timely communication builds trust.

Post-Project Debriefs

Once the project concludes, a post-project debrief can offer invaluable insights. This is not just an opportunity for the client to provide feedback but also for you to communicate lessons learned, potential areas for future collaboration, and to thank the client for their cooperation.

Mastering client communication is an evolving, ongoing process. Each client is different, and thus, your communication style may need to adapt. However, the fundamentals remain constant: clarity, honesty, and mutual respect are timeless pillars upon which successful client communication is built.

Chapter 10: Quality and Risk Management

10.1 Defining Quality in Manual Testing

Quality in manual testing isn't merely about ticking off a checklist or ensuring the software is free of bugs. The concept extends into the intricate fabric of the software development life cycle, influencing factors like performance, security, and user experience. Defining quality, therefore, involves identifying and aligning a range of variables and stakeholder expectations. Let's examine how quality is framed within the realm of manual testing.

Benchmarking Requirements

The starting point for defining quality is the requirements document. Whether it's functional specifications, user stories, or business requirements, this document serves as the benchmark for what the software is intended to achieve. In essence, quality is a measure of how well the final product aligns with these initial requirements.

Stakeholder Perspectives

Quality isn't a one-size-fits-all concept; it varies depending on who you ask. End-users prioritize usability and performance, developers may focus on code quality and maintainability, and business stakeholders could emphasize market fit and profitability. Therefore, defining quality requires reconciling these different viewpoints into a comprehensive quality model.

Operational Excellence

Operational aspects such as response times, load capacity, and resource utilization contribute to the overall quality. In manual testing, ensuring operational excellence means rigorously testing these metrics under various conditions to validate if they meet the specified requirements or industry benchmarks.

User Experience (UX)

No product can be deemed high-quality if it fails in delivering a good user experience. This involves aspects like UI design, ease of navigation, error messaging, and even micro-interactions that the user may have with the software. Manual testing, especially usability and exploratory testing, plays a pivotal role in gauging the UX quality.

Security and Compliance

Quality also encompasses the security of the software. This is increasingly critical in an era where data breaches and cyber threats are rampant. Compliance with regulatory standards like GDPR or HIPAA can also be a quality criterion that manual testing should validate.

Reliability and Consistency

A quality software product performs reliably under different circumstances and over extended periods. Whether it's the repeatability of test results or the consistency in user experience across different devices and browsers, reliability forms the cornerstone of quality.

Flexibility and Scalability

A high-quality software product is also one that is flexible enough to adapt to changes quickly and can scale as the user base grows. While these aspects may not be the primary focus of manual testing, they are crucial quality indicators that should not be overlooked.

Documentation and Traceability

Quality also extends to the testing process itself. Comprehensive documentation of test cases, test results, and any deviations from expected behavior are vital. Traceability matrices can link requirements to their corresponding test cases, ensuring that every requirement has been verified, thereby enhancing the quality assurance process.

Feedback Loops

The concept of quality is dynamic and evolves over time with user feedback and market changes. An efficient feedback loop, involving users, stakeholders, and the QA team, can significantly impact the perceived and actual quality of the software.

Conclusion

Defining quality in manual testing is an intricate, multi-faceted task that integrates various aspects ranging from functional correctness to user satisfaction. It serves as a composite metric that reflects the effectiveness of the entire development and testing process. Therefore, a well-articulated definition of quality is instrumental in guiding the manual testing effort towards delivering a product that not only meets but exceeds stakeholder expectations.

10.2 Risk Assessment Techniques

Risk assessment in manual testing is the structured evaluation of potential issues that could negatively impact the project. It's an indispensable aspect of test planning and strategy, providing a framework for identifying, quantifying, and prioritizing risks. Here's a detailed examination of various techniques commonly used for risk assessment in the manual testing landscape.

Risk Identification

The first step is to identify the potential risks. These could range from coding errors and security vulnerabilities to budget overruns and timeline delays. Multiple departments, including development, testing, and even marketing, should be involved in this phase to provide a holistic view of potential risks.

Risk Matrix

A risk matrix is commonly used to quantify and prioritize risks. The matrix plots the likelihood of a risk occurring against the impact it would have if it did occur. Risks that are both likely and high-impact are prioritized for mitigation.

Failure Mode and Effects Analysis (FMEA)

FMEA is a structured approach that involves identifying potential failure modes within a system and assessing the impact of each failure. For each identified risk, a Risk Priority Number (RPN) is calculated based on three factors: the likelihood of occurrence, the severity of the impact, and the ability to detect the failure. Higher RPN values indicate risks that need urgent attention.

Checklists and Templates

Using historical data and lessons learned from past projects, organizations often develop checklists and templates for risk assessment. These tools contain predefined risk categories and factors that should be considered, making the process faster and more systematic.

SWOT Analysis

Though generally considered a business analysis tool, SWOT (Strengths, Weaknesses, Opportunities, Threats) can be adapted for risk assessment. By evaluating these four dimensions in the context of the test project, one can uncover risks that may not have been apparent initially.

Expert Interviews

Subject matter experts and experienced team members can provide invaluable insights into potential risks, particularly those that are not immediately obvious. Their experience and expertise can help identify complex risks and their possible mitigation strategies.

Delphi Technique

In the Delphi technique, a panel of experts independently identifies and assesses risks. Multiple rounds may be conducted until a consensus is reached. This technique minimizes bias and relies on the collective wisdom of a group of experts.

Monte Carlo Simulation

While perhaps more common in automated testing or project management, Monte Carlo simulations can also be applied to manual testing scenarios. By simulating different outcomes based on identified risks and variables, this technique provides a range of possible outcomes and the probabilities of their occurrence.

Decision Trees

Decision trees help in visualizing the different paths that can be taken when a risk materializes and what the outcomes of those paths could be. This is particularly useful for risks that have a cascading impact, affecting multiple areas of the project.

Cost-Benefit Analysis

Once risks are identified and quantified, a cost-benefit analysis can be performed to evaluate the economic feasibility of mitigating them. This involves assessing the cost of implementing a mitigation strategy against the benefit gained from reducing the risk.

Understanding the array of techniques available for risk assessment allows the testing team to tailor their approach to the specific requirements and constraints of the project. The ultimate goal is to mitigate risks effectively without compromising on the quality or efficiency of the testing process. This aligns the testing efforts with the broader organizational objectives, making risk assessment not just a testing task but a strategic imperative.

10.3 Mitigation Strategies

Mitigation strategies in manual testing focus on minimizing the impact of identified risks on the project and ensuring that quality is not compromised. This entails implementing a range of techniques tailored to the risk landscape, effectively transforming the theoretical risk assessment into actionable steps. Here's an in-depth look at different mitigation strategies that can be employed in manual testing.

Risk Allocation and Ownership

Upon identifying and assessing the risks, allocating ownership to specific team members or departments is essential. Clear accountability ensures that each risk is actively managed, and timely actions are taken to minimize its impact.

Preventive Measures

The most straightforward mitigation strategy is to take steps that prevent a risk from materializing. For instance, if code complexity is identified as a risk, employing coding standards and conducting frequent code reviews can serve as preventive measures.

Test Prioritization

Risks with high impact and likelihood should be addressed first. The test cases that target these areas need to be prioritized. A focused approach to high-risk areas will ensure that the most critical aspects of the application are stable and functional.

Resource Allocation

For risks like resource constraints or skills shortages, the mitigation might involve reallocating resources to ensure that high-priority tasks are adequately staffed. In some cases, external hiring or contracting may also be a viable strategy.

Fallback Plans

Sometimes called contingency plans, these are devised to address the risk if it materializes. For example, if there's a risk of a third-party API being unavailable, a fallback plan might include having a mock API ready for testing purposes.

Regular Monitoring and Reporting

Risk mitigation is an ongoing activity. Regular monitoring is crucial to ensure that the mitigation strategies are effective and to identify any new risks that may have arisen. Transparent reporting mechanisms should be in place so that stakeholders are kept informed.

Checkpoints and Gateways

Implementing checkpoints at different stages of the project allows the team to assess whether the mitigation strategies are effective. Failing to pass a checkpoint could trigger a re-evaluation of the risk mitigation approach.

Communication Strategy

Effective communication within the team and with stakeholders can itself be a powerful mitigation strategy. Open, transparent communication ensures that everyone is aware of the risks and the steps being taken to mitigate them, thereby fostering collective responsibility.

Scheduled Reviews

A set schedule for risk review meetings can help in tracking the progress of mitigation strategies. These reviews serve as a forum for discussing the efficacy of the strategies implemented and making necessary adjustments.

Training and Skill Development

For risks related to skill gaps or new technologies, one mitigation strategy might be to invest in training programs. Upskilling the team not only addresses the immediate risk but also adds long-term value to the organization.

Financial Cushions

In case of financial risks, like budget overruns or unexpected costs, maintaining a financial cushion can be a practical mitigation strategy. This reserve fund can be allocated to address issues as they arise, without derailing the project.

Implementing a robust set of mitigation strategies involves a blend of proactive and reactive measures, fine-tuned to the project's specific needs. It's crucial to remember that risk mitigation is not a one-off task but a continuous effort that evolves with the project. Through vigilant monitoring, regular reviews, and adaptive strategies, manual testing teams can navigate the complex risk landscape, ensuring that the project stays on track and meets its quality objectives.

10.4 Creating a Quality Feedback Loop

Establishing a quality feedback loop in manual testing is pivotal for the ongoing improvement of both the testing process and the software product itself. This cyclical process captures information at various stages of the testing life cycle, analyzes it, and then feeds it back into the system for action. Below is an in-depth discussion of the steps and considerations involved in creating an effective quality feedback loop in manual testing.

Defining Quality Metrics

The first step in establishing a feedback loop is to define what "quality" means for the specific project at hand. This could be a combination of functional correctness, performance, usability, and other factors pertinent to the application. Metrics to measure these factors should be clearly defined and agreed upon.

Data Collection

Collect data from manual tests, including the number of defects, severity of issues, areas most prone to errors, and test coverage. This data serves as the raw material for your feedback loop.

Feedback Channels

Determine the channels through which feedback will be collected and disseminated. This could be through daily stand-ups, weekly reports, dashboards, or specialized review meetings. The channels should be accessible to all relevant stakeholders, including testers, developers, project managers, and even clients where appropriate.

Real-time Analysis

The value of a feedback loop is significantly amplified if the analysis is performed in real-time or near-real-time. Modern test management tools often come with analytical capabilities that allow you to monitor key quality metrics as the tests are being executed. This enables immediate action, reducing the time and effort needed for corrective measures.

Feedback Interpretation

Analysis should go beyond just numbers. Correlate the metrics with tangible aspects of the software and the user experience. Ask questions like, "What does a high defect rate in a particular module mean for the end-user?" or "How does the loading time affect the user's journey?"

Action Items

Based on the analysis, create specific action items aimed at improvement. These could range from code refactoring and additional test coverage to process changes like altering the test strategy or incorporating new testing techniques.

Communication and Collaboration

The effectiveness of a feedback loop is only as good as the communication channels it employs. Make sure that insights and action items are clearly communicated to the team and that everyone understands their role in implementing changes.

Iteration and Adaptation

After action items have been implemented, the loop starts anew—collecting data, analyzing it, and feeding it back into the system. Over time, this iterative process should lead to a refined testing strategy and a higher-quality product.

Review and Audit

Periodically, it's beneficial to review the entire feedback loop mechanism to check its efficacy. This can help identify any bottlenecks or inefficiencies in the system, providing an opportunity for further refinement.

Client and End-User Involvement

While often overlooked, incorporating feedback from clients and end-users can provide invaluable insights that internal teams might miss. This can be achieved through beta testing, user surveys, or direct client feedback.

Creating a quality feedback loop is an investment in the future of a software product. It ensures that the testing team doesn't operate in a vacuum but is continually aligned with the project's objectives and quality expectations. Furthermore, it lays down a foundation for a culture of continuous improvement, where learnings from each cycle are systematically used to enhance the next. This harmonizes the efforts of different stakeholders, from developers and testers to managers and clients, propelling the project towards its quality goals.

Chapter 11: Career Progression

11.1 Skill Development and Certifications

Skill development and certifications are vital aspects of career progression in manual testing. While experience in the field provides an in-depth understanding of testing practices and methodologies, formal training and certification bring structure, standardization, and validation to your skill set. Here's a focused exploration of how skill development and certifications can play a significant role in advancing your career.

Types of Skills Needed

In the realm of manual testing, skills can be broadly categorized into technical skills, domain-specific skills, and soft skills. Technical skills include understanding various testing types, using different testing tools, and having a strong grasp of the software development life cycle. Domain-specific skills are especially valuable when working in specialized industries like healthcare, finance, or e-commerce, as they offer a deeper understanding of what is to be tested beyond the software mechanics. Soft skills such as communication, problem-solving, and critical thinking are often underestimated but are critical for a tester to succeed.

Training Programs

There are multiple ways to acquire or improve these skills. Formal training programs, either online or in-person, offer structured learning paths that often culminate in a certification exam. These programs can range from beginner-level courses to highly specialized training on complex topics like security testing or data integrity validation.

Certification Benefits

Certifications, such as ISTQB (International Software Testing Qualifications Board) or CSTE (Certified Software Tester), serve multiple purposes. Firstly, they validate your skills and knowledge in manual testing, providing an objective measure of your capabilities. Secondly, they often serve as a differentiator in job markets where competition is stiff. Additionally, they offer a structured learning path, covering topics that you might have not encountered in your professional experience.

Skill Application in Projects

Upon acquiring new skills or certifications, the next crucial step is applying them in real-world projects. This not only enhances your learning but also demonstrates your improved capabilities to your employer or clients. It's beneficial to seek out projects or tasks that can specifically leverage your newly acquired skills.

Staying Updated

The tech world is ever-evolving, and what is relevant today may become obsolete tomorrow. Continuous learning is vital. Follow industry publications, blogs, and forums to stay updated. Webinars and conferences can provide insights into the latest trends and tools in manual testing.

Community Involvement

Engaging with the testing community, both online and offline, can also facilitate skill development. Sharing your experiences and learning from peers can provide practical knowledge that is often not covered in formal training.

Internal Training and Workshops

Within an organization, internal training sessions and workshops can be beneficial. These settings offer a more personalized learning experience and allow for direct interaction with instructors, who are often senior employees or experts in the field.

Skill Audits

Periodic self-audits can help you assess your skill set and identify areas for improvement. Online assessments, peer reviews, or even client feedback can serve as useful metrics for these audits.

Balancing Specialization and Versatility

While specializing in a particular type of testing or industry can make you an expert in that domain, it's also important to maintain a level of versatility. Having a broad skill set can make you more adaptable, allowing you to take on a wide range of projects.

Skill development and certifications are more than just resume boosters; they are tools for personal and professional growth. They provide a pathway for staying relevant in a fast-changing industry, while also offering avenues for career progression, whether it's moving into a more specialized role, transitioning into a leadership position, or simply becoming more proficient in your current role. The key lies in constant learning, practical application, and a commitment to excellence.

11.2 Networking and Building Professional Relationships

In the field of manual testing, professional growth isn't solely dictated by technical prowess or an impressive list of certifications. Equally important is the network of professional relationships you cultivate. The quality and extent of your network can directly influence your career trajectory, opening doors to new opportunities and enriching your work experience in various ways. In this section, we will delve into the crucial elements of networking and relationship-building in the manual testing community.

The Power of Connections

Knowing the right people can be invaluable. Whether it's a referral for a job opening, insights into emerging testing tools, or first-hand accounts of best practices within a specific industry, the benefits of a strong network are multifaceted. The very essence of networking goes beyond the transactional aspects; it's an investment in your long-term career and even personal development.

Channels for Networking

Multiple platforms and venues exist for networking in the field of manual testing. Industry events such as conferences, webinars, and seminars provide an opportunity to meet like-minded professionals. Online forums, LinkedIn groups, and community portals offer virtual spaces where testers can share knowledge and experiences. But don't overlook the power of everyday interactions. The workplace itself is a hub of networking opportunities; relationships with colleagues, supervisors, and even cross-functional teams can provide a treasure trove of professional benefits.

Best Practices

Networking is not just about exchanging business cards or sending a LinkedIn request; it's an art. Start by identifying what you can offer. Networking is a two-way street, and approaching it with a mindset of mutual benefit can set you apart. Active listening is crucial. When you focus on the needs and experiences of the other person, you not only gain valuable insights but also foster a relationship of mutual respect.

Follow-ups and Nurturing Relationships

Networking doesn't end once the conference is over or the LinkedIn connection is accepted. Relationships require nurturing. Simple gestures such as sharing an article that your connection might find useful, or a quick "hello" email every few months, can go a long way in strengthening the relationship. More formalized follow-ups, like quarterly catch-ups or annual reviews of mutual professional milestones, can also be incredibly beneficial.

Networking Across Hierarchies

Don't limit your networking to peers or immediate supervisors. Building relationships with industry leaders and experts can offer unparalleled learning opportunities. Mentorship from a seasoned professional can provide a significant boost to your career, offering insights that are rarely available through formal education or on-the-job training.

Internal Networking

Within your organization, there is also an internal network you can tap into. Departments other than your own will have unique perspectives and challenges when it comes to manual testing. The marketing team, for instance, can offer insights into customer behavior that can aid in your testing strategies. The developers can give you a heads-up about potential issues that only they would be privy to.

Relationships Beyond Work

Finally, let's not overlook the importance of friendships that go beyond the professional sphere. Many find that their most robust networking happens naturally and organically, built on genuine interests and mutual respect. The line between a professional contact and a friend is often thin, and there's nothing wrong with crossing it.

Networking is an ongoing process, not a finite project. As your career progresses, your network should expand and evolve along with it. It's a professional asset, valuable for its ability to open doors, foster learning, and create opportunities for collaboration and growth. Approach it with sincerity, manage it with care, and it will yield dividends throughout your career.

11.3 Moving into a Lead or Managerial Position

Climbing the career ladder in manual testing involves more than just technical acumen or years of experience. Transitioning from a hands-on testing role to a managerial or lead position is a significant shift that necessitates a broader skill set and a different mindset. In this section, we will explore the factors that contribute to successfully stepping into a leadership role in the realm of manual testing.

Recognizing the Need for Leadership Skills

First and foremost, recognize that a managerial role is not an elevated version of your current position. The competencies that make an excellent tester are not necessarily the same as those that make an effective manager. Leadership demands a mastery over people management, a skill that you'll need to develop alongside your technical expertise. Communication, problem-solving, and strategic thinking are fundamental in these roles.

Developing Soft Skills

While you'll still need to understand the intricacies of test plans, cases, and execution, soft skills like emotional intelligence, time management, and negotiation become increasingly critical. These skills will help you manage your team effectively, set expectations with stakeholders, and drive projects to completion. Engage in soft skills training, attend leadership workshops, and consider mentorship from someone already in a similar role to accelerate this development.

Certifications and Courses

Although not a strict requirement, managerial certifications can add credibility to your transition. Project management certifications such as PMP or Scrum Master can offer structured learning on how to handle projects from a managerial standpoint. While these are not focused on testing, the principles are often universally applicable.

The Transition Phase

The leap to management often occurs in steps rather than a single jump. You might first take on the role of a team lead, overseeing a small team while still being deeply involved in hands-on testing. This phase serves as both training grounds and a proving field for future managerial roles. You can assess your readiness and aptitude for leadership while gaining practical experience. It also allows your team and higher-ups to gauge your effectiveness in a leadership position.

Resource Allocation and Planning

As you move up, your focus will shift from test coverage and bug reports to resource allocation, budgeting, and strategic planning. Understanding the broader picture becomes crucial. You'll need to know how to distribute tasks among your team members to maximize efficiency and meet deadlines without compromising on quality. The knowledge you gained as a tester will still be in play but applied in a broader context.

Team Dynamics

In a managerial position, you'll need to foster a culture that encourages open communication, continuous learning, and mutual respect among team members. Your role will include resolving conflicts, facilitating team discussions, and ensuring that everyone is aligned with the project goals. You'll also be responsible for the professional development of your team members, including training, skill-building, and career progression.

Setting Up Metrics and KPIs

Effective management is often backed by data. As you step into a managerial role, one of your responsibilities will be to establish Key Performance Indicators (KPIs) and other metrics that will help measure both individual and team performance. These metrics will guide you in decision-making and offer quantifiable data to assess the quality of work.

Feedback Mechanisms

One of the cornerstones of effective management is a robust feedback mechanism. Regular one-on-ones with team members, performance reviews, and open channels for feedback will provide you with the insights needed to make informed decisions. These practices also contribute to a transparent work environment where everyone is clear about expectations and goals.

Staying Updated

Even as you move into management, keeping yourself updated on technological advancements and testing methodologies is essential. Your decision-making will need to be informed by current best practices, and you may still need to engage in hands-on work periodically.

Moving into a managerial or lead position is a multi-faceted transition requiring a blend of technical and soft skills. It offers new challenges and opportunities, requiring you to grow and adapt continually. As you evolve from being an individual contributor to a manager, your ability to steer your team effectively will not only shape your career but also significantly impact your organization's success.

11.4 Specializing Within Manual Testing

Specialization within the field of manual testing offers a focused career path that allows you to hone in on a particular aspect of testing, whether it's a type of application, testing methodology, or a specific industry. The value of specializing lies in your ability to become an expert in a niche area, setting you apart in a market that often rewards depth over breadth. Here, we'll delve into the factors that can guide you toward a rewarding specialization in manual testing.

Identifying Areas of Specialization

The first step toward specialization is identifying which areas interest you the most. The field is vast, covering various domains, from mobile and web applications to embedded systems and even industry-specific applications like healthcare or finance. Each has its own set of challenges and intricacies, requiring particular skills and knowledge.

Developing Expertise

Once you've chosen a focus area, the next step is to deepen your expertise. This process involves more than just reading articles or taking online courses. Attend specialized workshops, read seminal papers, and get your hands on any available case studies in the domain. The aim is to immerse yourself in your chosen specialization deeply.

Engaging in Industry Forums

Specialization can often lead to becoming a thought leader in your chosen field. Engaging in industry forums, whether online or through conferences, allows you to share your knowledge and learn from peers. This interaction often leads to opportunities for collaboration, research, and even job offers from organizations seeking your specialized skills.

Certification and Courses

Obtaining certifications can further establish your expertise. These qualifications serve as formal recognition of your specialized skill set and can make you more marketable. Several organizations offer domain-specific certifications, and while not all of them may carry the same weight, a certification from a recognized body can significantly bolster your credentials.

Consulting and Freelancing

Specialization opens doors to consulting roles where your expertise can be leveraged on a project-to-project basis. This path allows for varied and challenging work and can be financially rewarding. However, it also demands a high level of self-discipline and exceptional skills in project management and client communication.

Mentorship and Training

As a specialist, you're also likely to find opportunities for mentorship and training. Being able to guide others through the complexities of your specialization is rewarding and offers a different set of challenges compared to hands-on testing. Moreover, teaching is a powerful tool for consolidating your own understanding and skills.

Research and Development

With specialized skills, you can contribute meaningfully to research and development efforts. This work may involve investigating new testing methods, tools, or processes that can better serve your specialization. R&D roles are commonly found in larger organizations with the resources to invest in long-term research, but they can also be an aspect of consultancy or independent work.

Market Trends and Future Prospects

While specialization can offer several benefits, it's crucial to consider the market trends. Some specializations may have a limited scope or may become redundant due to technological advancements. Continuous learning and adaptability are key to ensuring that your specialization remains relevant.

Career Trajectory

As a specialist, your career trajectory may differ from a generalist. Your options for advancement might be more narrowly focused but can also lead to becoming a highly sought-after expert. You could move into senior roles within your specialization or transition into consultancy, training, or R&D.

Specializing within manual testing is a calculated move that offers both risks and rewards. The process requires dedication, continuous learning, and a passion for your chosen field. The depth of expertise you gain, however, will make you a valuable asset to any organization, offering a fulfilling and potentially lucrative career path.

Chapter 12: Adapting to Industry Changes

12.1 Upskilling to Stay Relevant

In a constantly evolving field like software testing, upskilling is not a luxury; it's a necessity. As technologies and methodologies adapt and evolve, the skills required to test them effectively must also transform. Staying relevant is a continuous endeavor, and here we will explore the aspects to consider when upskilling in the realm of manual testing.

Emerging Technologies and Techniques

One of the first areas to focus on when considering upskilling is identifying emerging technologies and techniques in the field. This might include new approaches to usability testing, updates to regulatory standards, or advancements in testing tools. Monitoring publications from thought leaders, attending industry events, and participating in webinars can provide insights into where the industry is headed. These resources can help pinpoint what skills you should focus on developing.

Skill Gap Analysis

Another essential step is conducting a skill gap analysis. This exercise helps identify the difference between the skills you possess and the skills currently in demand. Once you recognize these gaps, you can develop a focused learning plan. Many online platforms offer specialized courses in software testing, and formal education is also an option. Skill gap analysis should be an ongoing process, revisited at least annually, as the demands of the field are continually changing.

Training and Certification

Certifications can be particularly valuable in certain specializations within manual testing. Not only do they offer structured learning, but they also provide a tangible credential that can validate your skills. However, choose your certifications wisely, as not all are equally recognized or relevant. Some may focus more on theory without sufficient emphasis on practical applications, which could be a drawback in the fast-paced, hands-on world of manual testing.

Hands-on Experience

There's no substitute for hands-on experience. Concepts learned theoretically must be applied practically to be fully understood and internalized. Whenever possible, seek out opportunities to implement your new skills in a real-world environment. This could be within your existing role, through a job rotation, or by participating in open-source projects or freelance work that offers relevant experience.

Soft Skills

Don't underestimate the value of soft skills in the realm of manual testing. Communication, problem-solving, and collaboration are among the critical soft skills that testers should cultivate. These skills not only improve your efficiency but also facilitate better relationships within your team and with clients, enhancing the overall quality of your work.

Networking

Networking is another key aspect of staying relevant. Establish connections with professionals in your field and related areas. These relationships can provide you with invaluable insights, offer career opportunities, and sometimes even give you a different perspective that can be beneficial to your work. LinkedIn, industry conferences, and webinars are excellent platforms for networking.

Consulting with Mentors and Peers

A mentor or a peer can provide expert advice on what skills are crucial and how best to acquire them. If you don't already have a mentor, consider finding someone who has experience in areas you wish to upskill in. The lessons learned from their experience can be invaluable, providing shortcuts to gaining expertise and avoiding common pitfalls.

Fostering a Learning Culture

Lastly, cultivate a mindset of lifelong learning. Upskilling is not a one-time event but a continuous process. The most successful manual testers are those who maintain an insatiable curiosity and are always open to learning, whether it's from a formal training program, a peer, or even a failure.

The landscape of manual testing is not static; it's a dynamic field influenced by technological innovation and shifting methodologies. Upskilling to stay relevant is a fundamental aspect of career longevity and success. Prioritize areas that align with both your personal interests and the needs of the marketplace to ensure that you're investing your time and resources wisely.

12.2 Importance of Continuous Learning

In the world of software testing, the constant evolution of technology, methodologies, and customer expectations can render yesterday's best practices obsolete. Here lies the crux of why continuous learning is not just a buzzword, but an imperative for anyone involved in manual testing.

Adapting to New Methodologies

The software industry doesn't remain static; it evolves. Agile, DevOps, and other software development paradigms didn't exist a couple of decades ago, but today they are prevalent. As these methodologies emphasize rapid deployment and iteration, a manual tester's role has changed to adapt to these fast-paced environments. Keeping abreast of these changes through continuous learning ensures that you remain an asset to your organization and can contribute effectively to the testing cycle.

Regulatory Changes and Compliance

Understanding and adapting to new regulations is another arena where continuous learning is indispensable. Whether it's accessibility guidelines, data protection regulations, or industry-specific compliance criteria, failing to update your knowledge can result in software that's not just buggy but also illegal.

Tool Proficiency

While manual testing often does not require as many tools as automated testing, there are still numerous utilities at your disposal for test management, defect tracking, and so on. As these tools are updated or new, better solutions are introduced, testers should be comfortable switching to new platforms. This kind of flexibility is only possible with a commitment to continuous learning.

Quality Metrics and Performance Indicators

The ways in which we measure quality also change over time. Key Performance Indicators (KPIs) that were considered benchmarks five years ago might not be as relevant today. Learning how to measure and interpret new forms of data can be essential in assessing the health of a software product adequately.

Interdisciplinary Skills

Modern software products are increasingly interdisciplinary, often requiring some knowledge of data analytics, cybersecurity, and even marketing considerations like user experience (UX). While a manual tester doesn't need to be an expert in these fields, having a baseline understanding can substantially improve the quality and scope of testing.

Client and Stakeholder Expectations

The end-users and stakeholders are increasingly knowledgeable about software quality and have specific expectations. Continuous learning can provide you with the updated terminology and best practices needed to communicate effectively with these groups, ensuring their concerns are addressed and their feedback is appropriately implemented in testing processes.

Career Advancement

It's not just about keeping your current job; it's about career progression. Specialized skills in areas like security testing, data integration testing, or UX testing can set you apart from your peers. Additionally, management skills are necessary for those looking to move into supervisory roles. These aren't skills you learn once; they need regular updating and refinement.

Intellectual Curiosity as an Asset

While all these practical considerations for continuous learning are vital, the inherent value of intellectual curiosity should not be underestimated. An inquisitive mindset often leads to innovative problem-solving and can be one of the most rewarding aspects of professional development.

Continuous learning is not just a strategy; it's a mindset. It positions you not just as a passive recipient of changes in your field, but as an active, engaged participant in your own career. In a profession where quality is the ultimate goal, equipping yourself with an ever-expanding toolkit of knowledge and skills is perhaps the most effective quality assurance strategy you can employ.

12.3 The Intersection of Manual and Automated Testing

The intersection of manual and automated testing is akin to the confluence of two rivers, each bringing unique attributes to form a more robust and versatile waterway. Both manual and automated testing come with their individual strengths and limitations, and understanding where they intersect can create a more resilient, effective, and efficient testing ecosystem.

Complementing Each Other

Many people assume that the increasing automation in the software industry heralds the end of manual testing. This perception is far from reality. Automated testing excels in repetitive, time-consuming tasks, allowing quicker cycles and higher reliability for specific types of tests. However, it falls short in areas requiring human intuition, understanding of user experience, and complex decision-making. Manual testing, on the other hand, thrives in these areas. By recognizing the strengths and weaknesses of each approach, teams can employ a hybrid model that uses automation for what it does best, and relies on manual testing where human expertise is essential.

Shared Skill Sets

Understanding both manual and automated testing provides a more holistic view of the testing landscape. Skills like test planning, requirement analysis, and defect tracking are universally applicable. Learning scripting languages, even at a basic level, can be beneficial for a manual tester as it provides an appreciation of what can be automated, making the transition between the two smoother.

Common Tools

The integration of manual and automated testing often happens through shared tools. Test management solutions usually offer functionalities for both, creating a central repository for test cases, execution results, and documentation. This seamless integration makes it easier to manage complex projects that require a diverse testing approach.

Quality Assurance Versus Quality Control

While automated testing is excellent for quality control—ensuring that the code meets certain standards—manual testing often takes on more of a quality assurance role, shaping the software into something that not only works but also delivers a high-quality user experience. When manual and automated testing are effectively integrated, they offer a more comprehensive approach to both quality control and assurance.

Continuous Integration/Continuous Deployment (CI/CD)

In CI/CD pipelines, automated tests are generally run as part of the build process, but that's only one piece of the puzzle. Manual testing often comes into play before significant releases, after automated tests have ensured that the software is functionally sound but before it's exposed to the end-users.

It's a final checkpoint that benefits from human intuition and expertise, providing an additional layer of quality assurance.

Cost and Resource Optimization

Another intersection point is the efficient allocation of resources. Automated testing requires an initial investment to set up but saves time and money in the long run for certain test cases. Manual testing, while more time-consuming for repetitive tasks, is quicker to set up and can be more cost-effective for exploratory, ad-hoc, and usability testing.

Feedback Loops

One of the most effective uses of both manual and automated testing is the establishment of rapid feedback loops. Automated testing can provide quick feedback to developers, allowing for immediate corrections. Manual testing offers deeper insights, often revealing how different elements of the application work together and how they will be perceived by end-users.

Career Paths

For testers, understanding both manual and automated testing opens up more career opportunities. Some companies look for generalist testers who can perform both types of testing, depending on the project requirements. Others may value specialized skills but appreciate the versatility of a tester familiar with both approaches.

By understanding the intersection of manual and automated testing, you set yourself and your team up for success, optimizing resources, skills, and methodologies to deliver software that is both functional and delightful to use.

12.4 Future-Proofing Your Career in Manual Testing

In an industry where change is the only constant, future-proofing your career in manual testing requires a dynamic, proactive approach. The volatility of the tech world can make any skill set obsolete within a short span, but certain core principles and strategies can ensure that your career remains resilient amidst this ever-changing landscape.

Commitment to Continuous Learning

The first principle for future-proofing your career is to embrace lifelong learning. This goes beyond simply keeping up-to-date with the latest tools and frameworks; it involves cultivating a mindset of intellectual curiosity. Subscribe to industry journals, follow thought leaders on social media, and participate in webinars and workshops. Being in the know will help you anticipate industry trends and adapt your skill set accordingly.

Diversify Skill Set

Manual testing may be your forte, but it doesn't have to be your only skill. Expand your capabilities to include areas like automated testing, cloud technologies, or cybersecurity. By broadening your skill set, you can offer more value to your team and organization. Specializing in niche areas of manual testing such as usability, accessibility, or domain-specific testing can also enhance your job security and demand.

Mastery of Soft Skills

Technical prowess is indispensable, but soft skills are equally crucial for career longevity. Skills like effective communication, leadership, and critical thinking can set you apart from others in the field. For example, being able to translate complex testing issues into language that stakeholders can understand could make you invaluable to your organization.

Networking

Never underestimate the power of a strong professional network. Engage with peers, mentors, and industry experts. Participate in industry events, contribute to online forums, and don't hesitate to offer your expertise where you can. Networking can open doors for collaboration, skill exchange, and even new job opportunities.

Adaptability and Flexibility

Adaptability is the currency of the future workplace. The ability to pivot, to learn from failure and adapt your strategies, is invaluable. Whether it's a change in project scope, a shift in team dynamics, or the introduction of a new testing tool, being able to adjust and refocus quickly is an essential skill.

Certifications and Qualifications

While experience is invaluable, certifications can provide an extra layer of credibility. They act as an official endorsement of your skills and can make you more appealing in the job market. Don't just collect certifications for the sake of having them; choose those that will genuinely enrich your skill set and understanding of your field.

Contribution to the Community

Giving back to the community by sharing your knowledge can not only help others but also further solidify your own understanding and reputation. Writing articles, creating instructional videos, or giving talks on topics that interest you can establish you as a thought leader in the field of manual testing.

Financial Planning

While often overlooked, financial planning is an important aspect of future-proofing any career. Save diligently, invest wisely, and make financial decisions that provide you a safety net for any unpredicted industry downturns or job changes.

Personal Branding

Finally, develop your personal brand. Your reputation, online and offline, can play a massive role in your career trajectory. Keep your LinkedIn updated, contribute to meaningful discussions, and showcase your work and achievements.

The process of future-proofing your career in manual testing is continuous and multi-faceted. But if you regularly invest in your skills, adapt to changes, and plan carefully, you can significantly increase the likelihood of a long, fruitful career.

Appendix A: Glossary of Key Terms

Acceptance Criteria: Specifications that a software product must meet for the client to accept it. These are predefined conditions under which a product's functionality is assessed.

Bug: A flaw in the software that produces incorrect or unintended results. Bugs can vary in severity from minor to critical.

Black-box Testing: A testing methodology where the tester does not need to know the internal structures or workings of the application.

Cross-browser Testing: The process of verifying the functionality and design of a web application across multiple web browsers to ensure compatibility.

Data-driven Testing: A framework where multiple sets of data are used to either drive the same test or construct multiple tests.

End-to-End Testing: A methodology used to test whether the flow of an application is working as expected from start to finish.

Functional Testing: Type of testing that ensures that the system is functioning according to the defined specifications and requirements.

Heuristic Evaluation: A usability engineering method where a small set of evaluators examine user-interface designs to identify usability issues.

Integration Testing: Testing of combined parts of an application to determine if they function correctly together.

Load Testing: A type of performance testing aimed at determining a system's behavior under peak or excessive load conditions.

Manual Testing: The process of manually executing test cases without the aid of an automated tool.

Non-Functional Testing: Testing of software characteristics that are not related to specific functions or user actions, such as performance, security, or usability.

Quality Assurance (QA): The planned and systematic activities used to assure that quality requirements for a product are met.

Regression Testing: A testing practice to ensure that newly added features have not broken any of the existing functionalities.

Smoke Testing: A quick, preliminary test to reveal simple failures severe enough to reject a prospective software release.

Test Case: A set of conditions under which a tester will determine whether an application or software system is working correctly.

Test Plan: A detailed document that outlines the test strategy, resources required for testing, test schedule, and criteria that will deem the testing phase complete.

Usability Testing: A method to evaluate a product's user interface and overall user experience.

User Acceptance Testing (UAT): The final phase of testing, where the actual users test the software to confirm whether it can handle the required tasks in real-world scenarios.

White-box Testing: A testing methodology where the tester has knowledge of the internal workings, structures, and architecture of the application.

WCAG: Web Content Accessibility Guidelines, a set of guidelines aimed at making web content more accessible to people with disabilities.

Viewport: The visible area of a webpage on a display device.

Boundary Testing: A testing technique used to identify issues at the boundaries of input domains, such as the maximum or minimum acceptable inputs.

Exploratory Testing: An approach where test design and test execution happen concurrently without explicitly documenting test conditions, test cases, or test scripts.

Fuzz Testing: A type of testing where the system is tested by inputting random data, known as "fuzz," to check for crashes or vulnerabilities.

Gray-box Testing: A testing methodology that is a hybrid of Black-box Testing and White-box Testing, where some knowledge of the internal structures is used to guide the testing process.

Monkey Testing: A technique where the system is tested by providing random inputs to check for system crashes or unexpected behavior.

Negative Testing: Testing aimed to determine how well the system handles error conditions or invalid input data.

Pair Testing: A collaborative approach where two testers work together at one workstation to test the software.

Performance Testing: A type of testing conducted to evaluate the system's performance under varying conditions.

Sanity Testing: Quick tests run on the software build, usually after receiving a new build or after some changes in the code, to ensure that basic functionalities work as expected.

Session-based Testing: An exploratory testing technique where testing is broken down into sessions, each with a mission and a charter.

Stress Testing: A type of testing meant to evaluate the system's behavior under extreme conditions, such as high user load or low system resources.

Test Driven Development (TDD): A software development approach in which tests are written before the code that needs to be tested.

Test Environment: The hardware and software configuration where the testing will be performed. This includes the server where the software is installed, the database back-end, any client-end hardware, and any other software that interacts with the testing software.

Test Scenario: A high-level description of what needs to be tested in terms of functionality. Scenarios are more detailed than test procedures and less detailed than test cases.

Test Suite: A collection of test cases or test scripts that are intended to be executed together.

Traceability Matrix: A table that correlates any two baseline documents that require a many-to-many relationship to determine the completeness of the relationship.

Unit Testing: The smallest level of testing; used to test a small piece of code for correctness. Often automated but can also be conducted manually.

Validation: The process of evaluating a system during or at the end of the development process to determine whether it satisfies the specified requirements.

www.ingramcontent.com/pod-product-compliance
Lightning Source LLC
LaVergne TN
LVHW051743050326
832903LV00029B/2693